QUESTIONNAIRE SURVEY RESEARCH
WHAT WORKS

Linda A. Suskie
Assistant to the President for Special Projects
Millersville University

Association for Institutional Research
Resources for Institutional Research, Number Six

Second Edition

To order additional copies, contact:

AIR
114 Stone Building
Florida State University
Tallahassee FL 32306-3038
Tel: 904/644-4470
Fax: 904/644-8824
E-Mail: air@mailer.fsu.edu
Home Page: www.fsu.edu/~air/home.htm

ISBN 1-882393-05-8

Table of Contents

Preface

This book is designed for institutional researchers and others interested in research in higher education. It has two purposes: first, to provide the novice with a guide to the basic steps of survey research, and, second, to provide the more experienced researcher with a useful reference tool.

This book grew from my interest in survey research in general and in questionnaire design in particular. Many of the principles I learned in my graduate studies in educational testing and measurement can be applied to questionnaire design. After finding myself repeatedly answering the same questions from colleagues on survey research, I wrote a short manual. The manual grew into a series of workshops I have presented around the country for the Association for Institutional Research and a number of other professional organizations. Those workshops, in turn, inspired this book.

This monograph has been written in an informal style to keep it readable and interesting. A question-and-answer format has been used throughout to help you focus quickly on the point of the discussion and use this monograph as a reference. Rather than use citations, I admit freely to borrowing the thoughts and findings of many; they are listed in the "For More Information" section at the end.

The monograph has been organized in a roughly chronological fashion to take you step-by-step through the survey research process. Chapter 1 discusses planning the survey: determining the purpose of the study, collecting background information, designing the sample, and making a time line for completing the project. Chapter 2 introduces questionnaire design by discussing the pros and cons of various question formats. Chapter 3 is the central chapter of the monograph. It examines developing the questionnaire itself, and it is here that such important concepts as validity and reliability are introduced.

Chapters 4 and 5 deal more with the mechanics of conducting a survey. Chapter 4 addresses maximizing response rate, and such essential details as preparing a cover letter, pilot testing, and making follow-up mailings. It also briefly introduces in-person administrations, telephone surveys, and focus groups. Chapter 5 deals with preparing the returned surveys for data processing: editing and coding.

Chapters 6 and 7 discuss analyzing and reporting your findings. Chapter 6 is an attempt to cover several semesters' course work in statistics in a few pages that serve as a guide to choosing the most appropriate statistical analysis for your data and your needs. Those readers with some background in inferential statistics who need an easy reference guide should find it of value. Chapter 7 discusses reporting the survey results.

Although it might be tempting to read this book "as you go," it is strongly recommended that you go through the entire book and not just Chapter 1 as you plan your survey. Subsequent chapters will raise additional questions and ideas that will likely influence your plans.

This second edition is an expansion and update of the first. Sections on ethics, reliability, and validity have been added, along with brief comments on telephone surveys, focus groups, and in-person administrations. Many parts have been updated to incorporate the latest advances in technological support and several portions have been expanded, including the bibliography. Information on network and software resources have been added. Many other sections have been rewritten to improve their clarity.

Deep gratitude is expressed to those who contributed to the first edition of this book, including Sidney Micek, who conceived this monograph and proposed the initial outline and format, Jennifer Presley, Gary Reighard, Pat Terenzini, Lou Attanasi, and Tim Sanford. Special appreciation is expressed to Gary Hansen, whose thoughtful observations were incorporated into this second edition. Finally I would like to thank the many people around the country who have attended my workshops on questionnaire survey research, discussed their ideas and concerns with me, and shared examples of questionnaires with me. Many of their comments and questions have been incorporated into this edition.

This book is dedicated to my family: my husband Steve and my children Melissa and Michael.

Chapter I

Planning the Survey

Any good survey is a major research project, involving considerable time and resources. To make sure your efforts pay off, it's crucial that you spend some time planning. A survey that doesn't provide needed information or delivers it too late to have an impact is a tremendous waste. This chapter will help you delineate the survey's objectives, make some basic data collection and analysis decisions including selecting a sample, and set deadlines so everything gets done in time.

What is an Ethical Survey?

As professional researchers, we have an obligation and responsibility to adhere to the ethical and professional standards of our profession. The Association for Institutional Research's Code of Ethics is provided in Appendix 1. Other professional codes that apply to those engaged in survey research are the *Code of Professional Ethics and Practices* of the American Association for Public Opinion Research, the *Code of Professional Responsibility in Educational Assessment* prepared by the Ad Hoc Committee on the Development of a Code of Ethics of the National Council on Measurement in Education, and the Research Industry Coalition's statement on *Integrity and Good Practice in Marketing and Opinion Research*. Here are some key points from these standards:

- Strive to conduct a survey in a manner that is free of potential bias. Minimize potential sources of bias, and disclose factors that may bias the results of the survey.

- Protect the rights of privacy of those who are surveyed, and protect the confidentiality of individually identifiable information.

- Avoid harming, humiliating, embarrassing, or seriously misleading respondents.

- Avoid the fraudulent use of copyrighted materials.

- Take appropriate security precautions before, during, and after administration of the survey.

- Disclose the following items in any report of survey results:

    o   Who sponsored the survey, and who conducted it;

    o   The exact wording of questions asked, including the text of any preceding instruction or explanation to the respondents that might reasonably be expected to affect the response;

    o   A definition of the group being studied;

    o   A description of how the respondents were selected by the researcher; including eligibility criteria and screening procedures;

    o   Sample size and completion rates;

    o   Method, location, and dates of data collection;

    o   Information on the precision of the findings, including, if appropriate, estimates of sampling error, and a description of any weighting or estimating procedures used;

    o   A fair, objective, and complete presentation of the outcomes of the survey, both intended and unintended, without censorship;

    o   Appropriate attributions of the work and ideas of others; and

    o   Appropriate qualifiers for the conclusions of the research within the limitations of the study.

- Discourage others from making inappropriate reports, unsubstantiated claims, inappropriate interpretations, or otherwise false and misleading statements about survey results.

- Promote the use of multiple sources of information about persons or programs in making decisions.

Why Are You Doing a Survey?

It is the rare institutional researcher who decides (and has the time) to conduct a survey "just for the fun of it." Usually we conduct surveys because we perceive a need for the information it will elicit. Sometimes we are more explicitly asked to conduct a survey on a specific topic. In either case, the first step in planning a survey is to sit down with the people requesting the survey or needing the survey results to get more information on why a survey should be done. Seek answers to the following questions.

How will the results be used? What potential decisions will be affected by the survey results? Surveys are not ends unto themselves. They are tools that are used to help make decisions. You wouldn't buy tools for a workbench, or software for your computer, unless you knew for *what* you would use them, and unless you knew for sure that you *were* going to use them. Similarly, you shouldn't conduct a survey unless you know for *what* decisions the survey data will be needed, and unless you are convinced that you really *need* survey data to help make those decisions. Talk to the people who requested the survey and to anyone else who might use the results. Ask them how things will be different if the survey turns out the way they expect (or don't expect).

For example, suppose someone planned to conduct a survey on "institutional climate for diversity," and one of the questions asked respondents whether they agreed or disagreed that "Homosexuality is morally wrong." What could or would an institution do about this? Suppose it found out that 10 percent of the respondents felt this way? 30 percent? 50 percent? The very act of administering a survey raises the expectation that actions will be taken from the results. We do not want to generate results that we cannot respond to proactively. Don't conduct a survey on the need for child care services, for example, unless you are confident your institution would act upon strong indications that such services are needed. Ask whether the results of the survey will give rise to other needs, and whether those needs can be fulfilled.

Here are some other questions you might ask:

- If you ranked the various needs you have right now, where would this one (the need for information from this survey) fit?

- What are all the benefits that you and our institution might get from this survey?

- How important is this survey to you?

- Who is the audience for the results? Who are the people who will be most affected by the need for this survey or its results? Do they agree about the need? How will they react to the results and the solutions the results imply?

Sometimes, of course, a survey is needed for general background information and not to contribute to specific decisions. A periodic profile of the student body's goals and plans, for example, is helpful to the college administration and faculty in a wide range of contexts and not just for one or two specific decisions. In this case, you should still understand why there is a perceived need for the survey information and what uses will be made of the survey results. Will it be worth the time and resources spent collecting the information?

What are the objectives of your survey? State the objectives of your survey as specifically as possible. It's not enough to say you want to investigate student opinions on alcohol consumption. Refine the problem. Put your objectives in writing. If they're written down, they'll be clearer, easier to explain to others, and easier to keep in mind as you plan the survey. Keep in mind the "first golden rule of mathematics," sometimes attributed to John Tukey: An approximate answer to the right question is worth a great deal more than a precise answer to the wrong question.

What are the critical questions to be answered? You may find that to meet all the objectives on your list, you'll have to ask dozens or hundreds of questions. You'll have to drop some objectives from your list just to keep the process from getting too complicated. Talk again to the people who will be using the survey results. Find out what the most crucial decisions or objectives are. Of all the things people would like to know about this subject, which are the most important to them? What are the essential points that they want to find out no matter what? Why are they critical? Knowing the answers to these questions will be of great help in focusing the survey questions, deciding which are of primary importance, and making the survey of maximum value.

4

What information do you need to answer the questions? Write a list of the specific information—facts, figures, and opinions—that you will need to obtain to meet your objectives. Then ask how each piece of information will contribute to the survey's objectives. Be particularly critical of demographic information such as information on sex, age, racial or ethnic group, geographic origin, and marital status. Is it really important, for example, that you find out the sex of your respondents? Think about how you will use this information. Since men and women must be treated alike in many situations, your findings may be of no use and little interest to anyone.

What concepts need to be defined? To make sure your survey provides the needed information, some of the terms that you use will doubtless need clarification. If you're being asked to conduct a survey of students, press to find out exactly what is meant by "students." *All* currently enrolled students? Or just undergraduates? Just full-time undergraduates? Just full-time undergraduates living on campus? Just full-time undergraduates who entered as freshmen?

Words and phrases such as "attrition," "non-traditional student," "degree-seeking," "teaching effectiveness," and even "satisfaction" and "quality" are full of ambiguities. If such concepts are applicable to your study, define them to everyone's satisfaction *now*, before the study gets underway.

What have others done on this topic? Depending on the nature of the problem you are studying, a review of relevant literature and published survey instruments could be a considerable time-saver. Why reinvent the wheel when you can take advantage of what others have done before you? If the problem you're studying is student attrition, for example, a review of what others have found should help you hone in quickly on factors you should be examining. A review of surveys others have done on your subject will give you ideas on questions to ask and how to ask them. Try asking fellow institutional researchers at other colleges if you can adapt their questionnaires for your purposes rather than write your own from scratch.

Do you really need a survey? Ask yourself critically if you *really* need a survey to get the information you need. Perhaps the review of what others have done will suffice. Will your survey likely yield the same results that others have found? If so, is it worth the time and expense to conduct your own survey? Would a few phone calls or interviews give you all you need? If all you need is factual data, are you sure it isn't available from another source such as student records, tests, or direct observation? A great deal has been written in the assessment literature about *unobtrusive measures*: data that can be collected without having students complete a special survey or test. To see if you're meeting your curricular goals, you can count the number of books on various subjects checked out of the library. To assess writing skill, you can have students' senior papers blindly re-scored strictly for writing skill by writing experts. At the very least, much demographic information can usually be obtained elsewhere, rather than asking people through a survey.

What kinds of surveys *are* worth doing? If the information is needed for important decisions and there is no other way to get it, then you really do need a survey.

Is a survey the appropriate data collection method? If you need answers to sensitive questions for which you can't expect honest and valid answers (such as questions on racism, drug use, sexual activity), don't bother doing a survey—it will be extraordinarily difficult to have confidence in the results. If you need such information, either make inferences from published literature or hire a professional pollster with proven experience with sensitive surveys.

How will you analyze and report the data? What will you do with the information after you get it? Some data analysis constraints may be placed on your study depending on its purpose, computer availability, and the statistical sophistication of your users.

Is the purpose of your study to describe or explain? Many surveys are conducted simply to *describe* a group of people. Alumni surveys, for example, are often conducted to describe the alumni: their occupations, incomes, further education, residence, etc. Other surveys, however, are done to *explain, predict, or explore*. Why do some admitted freshmen choose not to enroll at your school? What types of students are most likely to drop out? What factors contribute to alumni career paths?

If your purpose is only to describe responses by summarizing them into totals and percents, then the information you collect can be in almost any form. If you are not planning on a large number of responses, these simple tallies may be made by hand without the help of a computer. Larger surveys may be summarized on a personal computer.

If you plan to explain, predict, or explore, however, you will probably need complicated statistical analyses such as factor analysis, regression analysis, or analysis of variance. These analyses require (1) knowledge of statistics, either your own or that of someone available to advise you, (2) a statistical software package such as SAS or SPSS and computer facilities large enough to handle it, and (3) the proper type of data. There are four basic data types or "scales" applicable to survey research:

Categorical or *nominal* data break people into categories. Examples of categorical data include racial/ethnic group, marital status, major, and responses to many multiple choice questions. Categorical data cannot be ranked and means or medians cannot be calculated. Because means cannot be calculated, these data cannot be used in many statistical analyses designed to explain, predict, or explore. Specifically, they cannot be incorporated into many *parametric* statistical analyses: analyses based on variation from a mean, such as t-tests, regression, analysis of variance, and factor analysis. You should therefore avoid collecting this type of data if you want to do more than describe.

Ranked, *ordered*, or *ordinal* data may be collected from questions asking for an "excellent/good/fair/poor" rating or similar ratings. Suitable analyses for ordered data are a topic of hot debate among social science researchers. Everyone does agree that medians can be calculated and that this type of data can be analyzed using *non-parametric* statistical analyses (those that use some other technique than assessing variation from a mean). Ordered data can therefore be used to at least a limited extent to explain, predict, or explore.

But is it appropriate to calculate means for ordered data and use them in parametric analyses? This is where the debate lies. For further discussion of this topic, see the section on Likert scales in Chapter 2.

Scaled or *interval* data can be converted into meaningful numbers, where the difference between, say, a 1 and 2 is the same as the difference between a 4 and 5. (Time, height, weight, grade point average, and salary are examples of scaled data.) Means can be calculated, and the data can be analyzed using a wide variety of powerful parametric statistical techniques. If you would like to use a fairly complex statistical analysis with your data, you should try to make the data interval.

Dichotomous data are data that have only two possible values (such as sex or full-time/part-time status). Although they are technically categorical data, because there are only two values in dichotomous data, they can be treated as scaled data. Categorical and ordered data can often be grouped into dichotomous categories and then introduced into a parametric statistical analysis.

If you plan to use statistical analyses to explain, predict, or explore and anticipate, keep in mind that you will get more meaningful results if your questions have a fairly large number of response choices. (Statisticians would say that the greater variability improves the explained variance.) Balance this against the difficulty that many people have in distinguishing among more than seven possible responses.

A final question to consider is who will use your findings. Unsophisticated users may not be able to understand or appreciate a factor analysis, even if you determine that it would best meet their needs. Simple tallies may be all that your users want.

Are Exit Surveys Worthwhile?

Every year it seems that hundreds of colleges across the country decide that they want to find out why some students drop out and that the way to find out is by doing an "exit survey": having the dropouts fill out a questionnaire or be interviewed either while they're in the process of "signing out" or a few months afterward. Don't do it! It's well-documented that these are the *worst* times to ask these students while they're leaving. When they're signing out, they're probably angry and frustrated, and your survey is just one more obstacle they face before they can leave. Just to get you "off their backs," many will give you one of two reasons for leaving: "financial difficulties" or "personal reasons." These "reasons" are probably only the symptoms, not the underlying problems. After these students have left, many are probably thoroughly disenfranchised from your school and difficult to track down, so you'll get a very poor response rate.

So how should you study the factors affecting student attrition? This method will yield far more useful, valid information:

1. Do a quick review of the literature on reasons why students drop out of college (some of the key researchers on this subject are Vincent Tinto, Ernest Pascarella, Patrick Terenzini, and Alexander Astin). You may get

so many ideas from this review that you may find you don't need to do a survey . . . at least not right away.

2. Use the material from your literature review to design a survey for freshmen and possibly sophomores (the students most likely to drop out). Design the survey to ascertain whether some of the factors you've picked up from your literature review are relevant at your college.

3. Conduct the survey using a random sample of currently enrolled students.

4. Hold the results until the beginning of the next academic year.

5. Determine which of your respondents are still enrolled, and collect relevant demographic data on all respondents (perhaps SAT scores, high school rank, and current grade point average, for example).

6. Conduct a statistical analysis (such as regression analysis or discriminant analysis) to determine which factors distinguish best between "stayers" and "leavers." (I've gone a step further and split the leavers into two groups: "voluntary" leavers and those who are "kicked out" for academic or disciplinary reasons.)

By collecting data from your dropouts while they're still enrolled and still connecting with your institution, and by having a data base of still-enrolled students to compare them against, you'll get much better results with this method than with exit interviews.

Should You Use a Published Questionnaire or Design Your Own?

With the recent explosion of interest in higher education assessment, there is a wealth of published questionnaires available on subjects such as freshman attitudes, student retention, faculty views, alumni satisfaction, and campus climate. Should you use one of these questionnaires or write your own questionnaire? It depends on four factors and their relative importance to you.

Relevance. This is the most important factor, because questions that don't interest you or that don't apply to your situation diminish the survey's validity. In this respect, the "homegrown" questionnaire usually wins: it will look at exactly what you're interested in and no more. A published questionnaire will probably include questions that your respondents find vague or confusing and will probably *not* include some of the questions that most interest you (although many questionnaires leave a few extra spaces for answers to "local" questions).

Validity evidence. It is often difficult and expensive to validate a "homegrown" questionnaire (ways to do this are discussed in Chapter 3). Published questionnaires sometimes have validity evidence available, although it may be of questionable merit. If validity evidence is important to you, request a "technical manual" of norms and validity and reliability evidence from the questionnaire's publisher. Show it to a faculty member with a background in education or psychology and get his or her opinion on its caliber.

Cost. A "homegrown" survey will probably have a lower cost in terms of hard dollars; participating in national surveys may cost as much as several thousand dollars. If you budget is tight, this may decide matters for you. But "homegrown" surveys also have their costs, mostly in terms of staff time for administering the survey, data entry, and processing. Many survey publishers will administer the surveys for you (by mail) and enter and process the results. If you have very limited staff resources, it may be that the only way you can get the survey done is to pay someone else to do it.

Comparative information. A "homegrown" survey will give you information on only one entity: your institution. In today's increasingly competitive climate, it's becoming more and more important to know how we stack up compared to other institutions of higher education. Participating in national surveys will often give you national or regional norms against which you can compare your institution. Beware, though, that some surveys' "norms" are of questionable merit: they simply consist of participating institutions and may not represent a representative cross-section of all institutions.

So which is better, a local survey or a published one? Both have their pros and cons. The best choice depends on your particular needs and resources. If your resources permit, both should be included in a comprehensive institutional research program.

Should You Hire a Contractor to Do the Survey or Do It Yourself?

Dozens of professional pollsters are available for hire to help you design, conduct, and analyze a survey. Should you take advantage of these services or do everything yourself? It depends on two factors and their relative importance to you.

Validity evidence. As noted above, it is often difficult and expensive to validate a "homegrown" questionnaire. A professional pollster may have more experience in validating a survey and may be able to collect validity evidence more efficiently than you can. Sometimes, the mere fact that a "professional" has done the survey will add credibility to the results, even if validity evidence *per se* is still limited.

Cost. A "homegrown" survey will probably have a lower cost in terms of hard dollars; using a professional may cost as much as several thousand dollars. As when you consider a published survey, if you budget is tight, this may decide matters for you. If you have limited staff, however, using a professional survey researcher may be the only way to get the survey done.

Keep in mind that the costs of using professional assistance are extremely variable, and with a little creativity you can keep them modest. Most expensive would be to have the entire survey done by an outsider—preliminary research, questionnaire design, pilot testing, survey administration, data entry and analysis, and writing the report. If you do not need all these services, see if you can contract for only those you need. Perhaps you need help designing and pilot testing the questionnaire but can handle the administration yourself. Perhaps you just need help with data entry and analysis. Limited services may cost hundreds rather than thousands of dollars and be worthwhile.

Many research universities have survey research centers; see if there is one near you. Such centers often have affordable rates. Sometimes they can "piggyback" a few of your questions onto a survey being done for another purpose at a greatly reduced cost to you. Find out also if a local market research firm would be willing to do the project as a "gift-in-kind" to your college. The firm gets to write off the project as a charitable contribution, your development office gets credit for a gift to your college, and you get your survey done for free. It can be a win-win situation for all concerned; talk to your development office.

If none of these options meets your needs, yet you feel you need professional help, there are other resources that won't cost a dime. The last section of this book, "For More Information," lists dozens of resources on survey research. And there is almost bound to be a faculty member on your campus with experience in survey research who would be glad to spend a few minutes answering your questions. Try the faculty in your social sciences, psychology, education, or business programs.

Whom Will You Survey?

Your next step in planning your survey is to identify the group you want to survey. While this may seem a simplistic question, it requires careful thought. Suppose you are planning a survey of alumni. Do you want to include people who are in your school's alumni files but never completed a degree from your school? Do you want to include those who earned only a graduate degree from your school? Do you want to survey *all* alumni or just those of, say, the last five years? Suppose you are planning a survey of the student body on possible attrition causes. Do you want to survey all currently enrolled students or just undergraduates? Or just full-time undergraduates? Or just full-time degree-seeking undergraduates? Or just full-time degree-seeking under-graduates who live on campus?

This is also an important question because the type of people you survey will affect the kinds of information for which you can ask. You cannot expect people with eighth grade educations, for example, to give you sophisticated opinions on complex economic issues. Teenagers will, through lack of experience, be relatively uninformed on many consumer problems like credit and budgeting.

Do You Need a Sample or a Census?

Most surveys in higher education involve contacting a *sample* or subgroup rather than making a *census* or survey of everyone. The major reason for this is cost effectiveness. Contacting a smaller group will save postage, printing, and data processing costs as well as time in assembling mailings and editing and coding the results. If the sample is carefully chosen and sufficiently large, these savings come with little sacrifice in terms of statistical accuracy.

It's also worth noting that a true census with a response from everyone is almost impossible to obtain. There will always be people with incorrect addresses and people who simply refuse to cooperate, so attempting a census will likely bring only a sample of responses, albeit a fairly large one.

There are two instances where you might attempt to contact everyone rather than take a sample. The first is if your entire group is relatively small. If your entire student body is only 450 students or if you have only 150 computer science alumni, go ahead and survey them all. The second instance is if your survey is on a critical, sensitive subject and someone influential might try to disparage the results because they are from "only" a sample.

How Many People Should You Survey?

The number of people you survey depends on the amount of "sampling error" you're willing to put up with. "Sampling error" describes the possible difference between your findings and the true results if you were able to obtain valid responses from *everyone*. For example, suppose you found that 35% of your students are planning on graduate study with a sampling error of 3%. This means you could be quite sure (actually 95% sure) that between 32% and 38% of *all* your students are planning on graduate study (i.e., 35% - 3% and 35% + 3%). It makes intuitive sense that the more people you survey, the smaller the sample error will be. The table below lists the sample size needed for each amount of sample error.

Random Sample Size	Sample Error
196	7%
264	6%
384	5%
600	4%
1,067	3%
2,401	2%
9,604	1%

While increased sample size reduces the sample error, you can see from the table that the benefits eventually diminish, especially beyond sample sizes of 1000 or so. Even professionally conducted national polls rarely sample more than 1000 people. For your purposes, you may be quite happy with a sample of 300 or so people. Let's say that 55% of your students are satisfied with your college. If you polled only 300 randomly selected students, you'd be right 19 times out of 20 about whether a majority of students are satisfied. You should rarely need a sample size more than about 500.

An important qualifier here: these figures assume a 100% response rate! Depending on your response rate, you will probably need to contact many more people to get the number of responses you would like. For example, if you would like 500 responses and expect a 50% response rate, you will need to survey 1000 people initially.

You may be wondering why no mention has been made of the overall size of the group from which you're sampling. Doesn't it make a difference? Not much, unless you're sampling from a group of less than 1000 or so.

Here are the sample sizes you need for 5% sampling errors from some relatively small groups:

Size of Group You're Sampling From	Sample Size
10,000	370
5,000	357
2,000	322
1,000	278
500	217
250	155
100	80

If you would like more information on calculating sample size and sampling error for small groups, see the Krejcie & Morgan or Scheaffer, Mendenhall & Ott references in the "For More Information" section in the back of this book.

A few final notes on sample size:

- If you want to study any subgroups (for example, just If you want to study any subgroups (for example, just freshmen or just students who withdraw or just business majors), either plan a larger overall sample size or realize that these subgroups may have a much larger sampling error. Very small subgroups may have such a large sampling error that no meaningful conclusions can be drawn about them.

- As noted earlier in this chapter, ethical standards require that you should report your sample size, your response rate, and the size of your sampling error when you report and interpret your results. Chapter 6 (Analyzing the Survey Data) will explain how to calculate sampling error.

How Will You Select Your Sample?

For your survey results to be meaningful, you will want your sample to be representative of the entire group from which you are taking your sample. Ideally, the best way to make sure a sample is representative is to choose it "randomly." In a random sample, every single person you'd like to survey has exactly the same chance of being drawn. The concept of randomness is what makes sweepstakes and lotteries fair (everyone who enters has an equal chance of winning the car or the trip to Europe or $40 million) and randomness is what makes a survey both fair and accurate. It lets you assume that your sample will closely resemble the entire group you are selecting from. The moment you stop being perfectly random in picking your sample, your sample error increases by an unmeasurable degree.

Simple random samples can be generated in a number of ways. The easiest way is by computer: if the group from which you want to sample (say, your undergraduate student body) is on a computer file, check if your computer software can select a random sample for you (many statistical packages can).

If your computer software doesn't have this capability, you can generate a random sample with the simple and reasonable assumption that the last two or three or four digits of each person's social security number (or other identification number or home telephone number if everyone in your group has one) are randomly assigned. Let's say you would like to sample 600 students out of 5000 at your school:

1.   Social security number (or telephone numbers) end in 10,000 possible four-digit combinations (0000 through 9999). Since you would like to sample 12% of your students (600 out of 5000), you would like to choose 12% or 1200 of the possible four-digit combinations.

2.   Using a random numbers table or by asking a few colleagues for digits, choose a starting number—say, 3892.

3.   Your random sample will consist of all students whose social security numbers end anywhere from 3892 through the next 1200 numbers, up to 5092. If you computer cannot list these people for you, a student or clerk can go through a listing and identify the sampled students with a highlighting pen.

There are other ways to obtain random samples:

Systematic random samples involve taking every tenth, 50th, or other like-numbered person from a list. While this approach is simple, you may run the risk of omitting key components from your sample. Let's say you are sampling 200 names from a 1000-page phone book and you decide to choose the first name on every fifth page (page 5, page 10, etc.). But maybe in your town there is a sizable group of strong German descent, mostly active and opinionated about your school. There are therefore a lot of names in the phone book beginning with "Sch." They start with the second name on page 750 and run through the last name on page 754. None of these people has even a *chance* of being sampled!

Stratified random samples involve breaking your entire group into subgroups and then taking a random sample of each subgroup. This ensures that even small subgroups (such as minority groups, small majors or non-traditional students) are represented, so it is a good choice when you are focusing on differences among subgroups. If this is the major intent of your survey, you may want to have the same sample size for each subgroup. If the groups are not naturally the same size, the smaller subgroups will need to be over-sampled while the larger subgroups are under-sampled.

Cluster random samples involve taking a random sample of groups or "clusters" and then surveying everyone in those clusters. For example, you might take a random sample of freshman English classes and survey everyone in those classes. Or you might take a random sample of dormitory floors and survey every-one on those floors. Cluster samples are particularly useful when you plan to distribute a questionnaire in person.

All random sampling techniques assume that you have a complete and accurate list of all the people from which you wish to select your sample. In reality, this is rarely the case. Alumni files, for example, are notoriously incomplete. Even rosters of currently enrolled students always include a few students with missing, incomplete, or outdated addresses. Surveys administered to a class in person will miss absent students.

This problem becomes particularly serious when you are trying to survey the public at large, as you might in a "community needs" assessment. There is usually no complete, accurate list available of the people from which you wish to choose your sample. Many people rely on telephone directories, which omit people with unlisted numbers, people who have recently moved, and any adults in a household who do not have a listing in their names (depending on the policy of the telephone company in your area, this could include many married women, who might be an important target for you). Voter registration rolls have similar limitations. There is no way around this problem, except to recognize it and note it as you plan your survey, analyze the findings, and report your results.

There are some instances when a non-random sample is appropriate. Sometimes the list of the group from which you wish to sample is so incomplete that even selecting randomly from it would give you a biased sample. Sometimes the list is not easily accessible (for example, students with some special characteristic that is not on their computer records). Sometimes it takes too long to obtain the list (perhaps there's a long waiting list for computer services). Non-random samples may be appropriate in these instances. Non-random samples can be valid, unbiased samples, but the burden of proof is on you to demonstrate that they are.

There are two basic types of non-random samples. A *judgment* sample is carefully chosen so that, in your best judgment, it is representative of the entire group. National "test markets" are chosen this way. You might use judgment sampling to select a focus group or a panel. A *convenience* sample is just that—a sample chosen because it is easily accessible. If you ask a few faculty you're friendly with if you can borrow their classes for ten minutes to administer a survey, you're choosing a convenience sample.

What Survey Design Should You Use?

Much of the research in higher education consists of conducting *one* survey of *one* sample of people and describing (or perhaps explaining or exploring relationships among) the results. Before you decide to do this yourself, consider other possibilities. Your choice will depend on the purposes of the study and time and monetary constraints.

One possibility is to survey *more than one* group and compare results among groups. You could, for example, compare students who graduate with students who fail to graduate, business majors with education majors, men with women, freshmen with sophomores, last year's graduates with graduates of ten years ago.

Another possibility is to examine changes in one or more groups *over a period of time*. This is called a *longitudinal* survey. You might want to survey freshmen and then survey the same students four years later to assess changes in attitudes or goals.

If you think a more complex design might be best for you, consult a faculty member from a social sciences, psychology, or education department for advice on the most appropriate research design.

Should the Survey Be Anonymous?

Professional standards dictate that most surveys should be *confidential*: results are processed and reported in such a way that individual responses cannot be identified. Indeed, some respondents will refuse to participate unless you guarantee the confidentiality of their responses. Unless you have good reason to report individual responses *and* you tell your respondents up front that you will be doing this, you should conduct a confidential survey and assure your respondents that their individual responses will be kept confidential and secure.

Some potential respondents may not be satisfied with your guarantee of confidentiality. They may be afraid to share their views unless completely anonymously, on a questionnaire that provides no information on the answerer's identity.   Some researchers therefore feel a survey must be conducted anonymously, not just confidentially, to ensure a good response rate.

Should your survey be conducted totally anonymously or should you simply assure your respondents of complete confidentiality?   This is not a simple decision to make. It depends on four things:

The nature of your questions.   The presumed advantage of an anonymous questionnaire is that it will increase respondents' chances of answering your survey and of answering it *honestly*. How important this is to you depends on the nature of the questions you are asking. A questionnaire dealing with sexual habits or political preferences may require anonymity much more than one asking about gardening activities.

The people you are surveying.   Will they be sympathetic with the goals of your survey or suspicious of your motives?   With a group of well-educated people familiar with the nature of your work, you may not need an anonymous questionnaire to get the response rate you desire.

How much factual information you need.   If you want to break down your responses by sex, age, socioeconomic status, or other variables and you already have access to such information, you may find a questionnaire that identifies the respondent is preferable for two reasons. First, you won't have to ask for such factual data on your questionnaire, shortening it and thereby increasing your response rate.   Second, by collecting your factual data from an original source rather than asking for them to be self-reported, you increase their accuracy. Some people may not remember their high school rank or annual income, for example, while others may choose not to respond to such questions.

The importance of follow-up mailings.   With a mailed, anonymous survey, you lose any chance of following up with a second mailing to those who don't respond the first time.   Since follow-up mailings can account for half of your total responses, this may be a serious problem. On the other hand, if you're distributing a survey in person this may be an unimportant consideration.

The disadvantages of anonymous surveys frequently outweigh their advantages, especially when they are mailed. You will find that professionally conducted surveys are usually identified in some way. Try to make your questionnaires as anonymous as possible by number-coding each rather than identifying it by name.

Do everything you can in every other way to motivate the respondent to answer and make up for any diminished response rate.

How Much Will It Cost?

Few of us have an open-ended budget. The rest of us need to consider how extensive a project we can undertake given our funds. In planning a budget for a survey research project with a mailed questionnaire, consider the following possible expenses:

Personnel time, including your time, your staff's time, and the cost of any special help (e.g., student workers, graduate assistants) brought in specifically for this project (see Appendix 2 for a sample list of the tasks that require personnel time).

Paper and envelopes.

Printing the questionnaire, cover letter, return envelope, and outer envelope in sufficient quantity to cover follow-ups as well as the initial mailing.

Postage for the initial and follow-up mailings (including postage for the envelope in which the survey is returned to you). These costs vary depending on whether you mail first class or bulk rate and how heavy the items are.

Incentives (e.g., a pencil, a quarter, a gift certificate to be given away in a drawing). These are discussed in Chapter 4.

Follow-up costs other than printing and postage, including telephone calls and certified mailings.

Data entry and processing costs.

Duplicating and distributing the final report.

With a mailed questionnaire survey, the biggest expense is usually postage, followed by printing. With a telephone survey, these costs diminish but costs for telephone use and personnel to make the calls can escalate. There is no general rule of thumb for estimating the cost of doing a survey; it varies according to individual circumstances. The three interrelated parameters are time, quality, and money (the more time and money you spend, the better the quality of the results). *You cannot get a good response rate and high-quality (valid) results without spending time and money.*

Should Your Survey Be Reviewed by an Institutional Review Board?

Federal regulations (specifically, 45 CFR 46, Subparts A-D) require research with human subjects to meet four criteria: (1) risks to subjects must be minimized, (2) risks to subjects must be reasonable, (3) selection of subjects must be equitable, and (4) informed consent must be sought where appropriate. Institutional review boards (IRBs) must be established to ensure that research meets these criteria, protects the rights and welfare of human subjects, and poses no significant risk or threat to their rights and welfare. There are three levels of review: full review (which requires appearing before the entire IRB), expedited review (in which at least one member of the IRB reviews the research plan), and exempted from review (under which the research plan must still be sent to the IRB).

Should your research be reviewed by this group? Probably not. "Internal" research for administrative purposes is exempt, and research that poses "minimal risk" to the subjects—no more than their "risk in everyday life"—and maintains and protects confidentiality need not be reviewed.

The legalities of IRBs have grown considerably more complex over the past few years. If you have any questions about this, speak with the chair of your institution's IRB, which is responsible for providing information.

When Will You Get It All Done?

The final step in the planning process is to determine when the information will be needed for decisions and to work out a time line ensuring that everything will be done by then. If your report is not available when decisions must be made, all the time and energy put into the survey will have gone for naught.

Make a list of all the things you will need to do to complete the project. For each item, note (1) when it must be completed, (2) how long it will take to do, and (3) when it must be started. Chapter 4 (Conducting the Survey) discusses the timing of the survey administration. Note which dates are flexible. You may need to trim your survey if you cannot complete it by your deadline.

A GANTT or PERT diagram may be helpful in planning the time line for your survey. If you are not familiar with these techniques, the staff of your computer center or your engineering faculty may be able to help you.

Appendix 2 gives an example of a time line for a survey research project.

How Can You Deal with Institutional Politics?

You may feel a variety of uncomfortable pressures at your institution, including pressure to:

- Do a survey without spending any money;

- Do a fast survey;

- Do too many surveys;

- Do a biased or invalid survey.

The response you can make to these pressures depends, frankly, on your campus culture and campus perceptions of you and your position. If you are highly esteemed on your campus as an outstanding research scholar, people probably listen when you explain why it's ill-advised to undertake a particular survey in a particular fashion. On the other hand, if you're viewed as a "number-cruncher" and someone in a powerful position is dictating what you are to do, you're in a more difficult situation (assuming you want to keep your job!). Following are some possible strategies:

Show the powers-that-be a cost breakdown (dollars, staff, computer resources). They may be able to help creatively solve the cost problem (for example, by providing student volunteers and outward WATS lines to conduct a telephone survey).

Show the powers-that-be your time line. They may be able to free up some staff to assist you with envelope stuffing, data entry, etc., to help move things along.

Explain to those with an "ax to grind" that you want them to have a good, useful survey that can't be attacked by others. Point out that people often attack the results by attacking the process. By having a valid, unbiased survey, discussion can focus where it should: on the results and their implications.

Document your concerns in writing.

Change your role from "doer" to "adviser." If you're asked to do a survey that will clearly run into serious problems, explain tactfully that you'd love to help, but you're overwhelmed with work and just don't have time to conduct the survey. You'd be glad, however, to review questionnaire drafts and offer advice on any other aspect of the survey process. This brings you a step away from the survey and lessens the chance of fingers pointing at you.

If your concerns about the survey amount to blatant ethical violations and you have enough courage, refuse to do the survey, citing relevant professional standards.

In your report, if absolutely all else fails and you are basically ordered to conduct a survey against your better judgment, point out the survey's flaws (tactfully) and note that the results should be viewed with caution.

But these things aren't going to happen to you! You're going to do a great survey! How? Let's start writing the survey questions in the next chapter.

Chapter 2

Formats for Survey Questions

Once a survey has been planned, the first step in developing the questionnaire is to construct questionnaire items that will get you the information you want.

This chapter will describe some formats for survey questions. The next chapter will discuss drafting individual items and integrating them into a questionnaire.

Yes/No Questions

Yes/no questions are questions with only two possible answers. Here are examples of questions that some researchers might pose as yes/no questions.

> Are you registered to vote?
> Do you support the legalization of marijuana?
> Are you a full-time college student?
> Do you use a personal computer?

The two possible answers are provided along with a space to indicate the chosen answer.

Advantages. As discussed below, yes/no questions lend themselves to a wide variety of data analyses.

Disadvantages. For two reasons, yes/no questions should rarely be used. First, very few questions are purely yes or no; most have a grey area in between. Consider the sample questions above. A person may be registered to vote but in another state. He or she may support the legalization of marijuana in certain circumstances but not others. He or she may have been a full-time student for the past three years but is attending part-time this semester.

Second, yes/no questions are not very interesting, either to the researcher or to the respondent. All they will tell you is how many people said yes and how many said no. They will not tell you why. Also, they may be boring enough to the respondent to make him or her throw the whole questionnaire into the circular file.

To salvage a yes/no question, you can make it more interesting by making it part of a "contingency question" such as this one:

> Are you attending college full-time or part-time this fall?
> ___ Full-time. Go to Question 9.
> ___ Part-time: Please rate your satisfaction with the following:

Contingency questions have disadvantages, however, as discussed in the next chapter.

How to analyze responses. Yes/no questions lend themselves to a wide variety of simple and complex data analyses. If you simply want to *describe* your results, you can compute the percent who said yes and the percent who said no.

The results of a yes/no question can also be included in a more complex analysis. For example, you can use the results to break your respondents into two groups (in the examples above, full-time vs. part-time or supporting/not supporting the legalization of marijuana). You can then compare how the other responses of these two groups differ from one another.

Yes/no responses are dichotomous data (data with only two possible answers, as discussed in Chapter 1). Responses can therefore be considered scaled data and included with other responses in parametric analyses such as analysis of variance or regression analysis. (Parametric and non-parametric analyses are defined in Chapter 1.)

How to report results. The easiest way to report the results of yes/no questions is to type onto a copy of the questionnaire the percent choosing each response. Round percentages to the nearest whole number.   Graphs are usually inappropriate unless you are comparing responses to several questions; the statistics are so limited that a graph will not be interesting.

Multiple-Choice Questions

Multiple-choice or fixed choice questions consist of a question or "stem" followed by a set of answers that the respondent chooses from:

> What is your one main source of financial support while attending college?
> ___ My own earnings and savings
> ___ My parents
> ___ Financial aid and loans
> ___ Other (please specify: _____)

Advantages. Multiple-choice items are widely used, principally because they are quickly and easily answered and the responses are generally easy to tally. They are particularly good for collecting factual information.

Disadvantages. The chief difficulty in writing multiple-choice questions is making sure you have included *all* possible answers. If you're not sure you've mentioned every possibility, you can use an "Other—please specify" response, but don't use it to salvage a poorly written question. Pretest the item as an open-ended question and use the most frequent answers as your responses.

Another problem with multiple-choice questions is that respondents will often check more than one answer, even if you don't want them to. Your coding, analysis, and interpretation will be a lot harder if you allow multiple responses. Try to make clear in your directions that only the *one best* answer should be marked. If a few respondents still persist in marking two or more answers, as you edit your responses choose one randomly (e.g., flip a coin) and discard the rest.

A third limitation of multiple-choice questions is that the data they yield are usually categorical or ordered which, as discussed below, can seriously limit your data analysis options.

Tips on writing. Here are some suggestions for writing multiple-choice questions:

- The stem should ask a complete question, even if it is phrased as an incomplete statement. The respondent shouldn't have to read the responses to figure out what you're asking, as they would with, for example, "The library is:".

- Limit the number of possible choices to five or six. It's hard for most people to keep more than that many in mind.

- Your choices should all be mutually exclusive (i.e., clearly distinct and separate from one another).

- If there is a dominant response that you're not interested in, include it in the stem (for example, "Aside from housing, what...?").

- Order the responses logically—numerically if the answers are numbers, for example. This helps people who know their answer find it quickly. (If your set of responses is a list of numbers, most people will pick from the middle of the list.)

- "Stack" your responses *vertically*, with the boxes or spaces to be checked in a column on the left. This saves confusion and searching for the right space to mark.

How to analyze responses. If you simply want to *describe* your results, you will probably want to compute the percent who chose each option.

Sometimes multiple-choice responses are ranges of figures, as in the example below:

> How many hours did you study last week?
> ___ 0
> ___ 1-3 hours
> ___ 4-6 hours
> ___ 7-10 hours
> ___ More than 10 hours

While you cannot compute an exact mean or median response for this item, you can compute an *estimated* median. To learn how, find a basic statistics textbook that explains how to compute medians from a grouped frequency distribution (such as Hays; see citation in the "For More Information" section at the back of this book). The estimated median can then be included in some of the non-parametric statistical analyses for ordered data that are described in Chapter 6.

Because multiple-choice questions usually yield categorical data, however, their results are usually difficult to include in complex parametric analyses such as analysis of variance, regression, or factor analysis. One way to use multiple-choice data is to break your respondents into groups based on their response. You could use the financial aid item given at the beginning of this section, for example, to break respondents into four groups: those whose main source of financial support is their own earnings and savings, their parents, financial aid and loans, and other. You could then use analysis of variance to compare how other responses of these four groups differ from one another.

Another way to use multiple-choice data is to code responses to them as a series of dichotomous (yes/no) responses. Responses to this question, for example,

> Where do you live?
> ___ In a campus dorm
> ___ At home
> ___ Off campus in a rented house or apartment

could be coded as responses to three yes/no questions: Do you live in a campus dorm? Do you live at home? Do you live off campus? A respondent living off campus would be coded No-No-Yes. These responses would be dichotomous data that can be considered scaled data. Some researchers are therefore comfortable including these data in parametric analysis such as regression analysis and factor analysis. Other researchers, however, point out that these data are not *independent* of each other (if the answer to the first option is "yes," the other answers *must* be "no"), and independent data is technically one of the prerequisites for these kinds of analysis. If you have any questions about whether this kind of treatment of multiple-choice data is appropriate in your situation, discuss the matter with a faculty member experienced with statistics and research design.

How to report results. The simplest way to report the results of multiple-choice questions is to type onto a copy of the questionnaire the percent choosing each response (and the percent who gave no response, if applicable). Percentages should be rounded to the nearest whole number. As noted above, with some multiple-choice questions you may be able to compute an estimated median, and this may be more interesting to your readers than the percent choosing each category. Multiple-choice results can also be presented in a bar or circle graph.

If the response choices are more than a word or two, the text will be easiest to present in a bar graph with horizontal bars.

Checklists

A checklist is a variation of a multiple-choice item in which respondents may choose as many responses as they like rather than the one best response.

> Please check all the reasons you decided to go to college.
> ___ To learn more about things that interest me.
> ___ To be able to get a better job.
> ___ To be able to make more money.
> ___ My parents wanted me to go.
> ___ I wanted to get away from home.

Advantages. As with multiple-choice items, checklists are quickly and easily answered and the responses are generally easily to tally.

Disadvantages. As with multiple-choice items, it is difficult to be sure you have included all possible answers, and the data are categorical or ordered, which limits your data analysis options.

Another problem is that some respondents will check many items, while others will check only one or two. The "heavy checkers"' responses will be carry more weight in the aggregated results; some think this is an unfair advantage they have.

But perhaps the greatest concern I have with checklists is that you get no sense of the relative importance or frequency of each item checked. If one student checks three reasons in the example above, we have no idea of the relative importance of each of those reasons. They may all be equally important, or one reason may be far more important than the other two.

Tips on writing. The suggestions given above for writing multiple-choice questions also apply to checklists.

How to analyze responses. Checklist responses must be coded as a series of dichotomous (yes/no) responses. In the example above, the question would be coded as answers to five separate questions: 12A, 12B, 12C, 12D, and 12E. A respondent choosing only the first two options would be coded Yes-Yes-No-No-No. (Data entry is discussed further in Chapter 5.)

If you simply want to *describe* your results, you will probably want to compute the percentage who chose each option, noting that the percentages will sum to more than 100% because more than one answer could be chosen.

As noted in Chapter 1, the responses are dichotomous data that can be considered scaled data and included in parametric analyses such as regression analysis and factor analysis.

How to report results. As with multiple-choice questions, the simplest way to report the results of checklists is to type onto a copy of the questionnaire the percentage choosing each response. Percentages should be rounded to the nearest whole number. Checklist results can also be presented in a bar graph. If the response choices are more than a word or two, the text will be easiest to present in a horizontal bar graph.

Rankings

In a ranking item, the respondent is asked to number all responses according to specified criteria:

> Please rank each category below to indicate how important it is to you as a source of financing. Rank the most important source "1," the second most important source "2," etc.
>
> ___ Full- and/or part-time work
> ___ Savings
> ___ Parental aid
> ___ Grants (e.g., Pell)
> ___ Loans
> ___ Scholarships
> ___ Veterans' benefits
> ___ Social Security benefits

Advantages. The primary advantage of rankings is that many respondents can easily understand them.

Disadvantages. Rankings have four serious weaknesses. First, they can be tedious to complete. Often a respondent must reread the list over and over as he or she is ranking it.

Second, rankings often incorrectly assume that respondents feel differently about every item on the list; this is often not true.

Third, rankings give very limited, incomplete information, making the results difficult to interpret. Consider one respondent's response to the following item:

> Please rank the reasons you decided to attend Clarendon College, giving a "1" to the most important reason and a "5" to the least important reason.
>
>   __1__   Academic reputation
>   __5__   Social reputation
>   __4__   Geographic location
>   __3__   Unique programs of study
>   __2__   Cost

You will never know if this respondent felt that "Academic reputation" was far and away the most important reason or if "Academic reputation" and "Cost" were virtually equally important. Even more significantly, you will never know if "Academic reputation" was *the* most important reason or just the best of the choices given here. Similarly, you will never know if "Social reputation" was not a factor in the decision to attend Clarendon, or just the least important of five very important factors.

Fourth, as discussed below, rankings are difficult to statistically analyze and interpret.

Because they have so many limitations, I do not recommend using rankings. Using rating scales, which are discussed later, will give you much more useful data.

Tips on writing. The key to writing a good ranking item is to make sure your directions are complete and that the criteria for the ranking are clearly specified.

Don't just say, for example, "Rank the following giving a 1 to the best and a 10 to the worst." Define in what respect you mean "best." Other tips: keep the list of items to be ranked no longer than ten items, keep them all on one page, and make clear whether you want *all* items ranked or just, say, the top three.

How to analyze responses. As noted above, one of the challenges of ranked data is figuring out how to analyze the results. If you compute the percentages who assigned each ranking to each response, you will be overwhelmed with numbers—especially if a long list is being ranked. Instead, you may simply want to compute the percentages who chose each response as their first choice, or perhaps one of their top three choices. The drawback to this method is that you're losing some of the ranking data your respondents provided.

Some researchers analyze rankings by figuring a mean or median ranking for each item. For example, suppose that 150 students responded to the "reason attending" item above. Thirty gave "Academic reputation" a ranking of "1," 45 gave it a ranking of "2," 60 gave it a ranking of "3," 10 gave it a ranking of "4," and 5 gave it a ranking of "5." The mean ranking would be 2.4; the median ranking would be 2.5. Note that means can only be computed for scaled (interval) data, and you probably have no assurances that the intervals between various rankings are equal. Many researchers therefore discourage computing mean rankings.

Because rankings yield only ordered data, not scaled, your data analysis choices are limited to non-parametric statistics. For a review of analyses appropriate for ordered data, see Chapter 6.

How to report results. Rankings are not only difficult to analyze, they are also difficult to report succinctly and effectively. Probably the simplest way is to give the median ranking of each response. Note that some readers will confuse the concepts of "ranking" and "rating" and instinctively expect the higher-ranked items to have higher medians. Depending on your audience, you may therefore want to consider recoding the rankings, changing (in the example above) a "5" to a "1," and "4" to a "2," and so on. If you do this, you will need to make clear that *higher* figures mean *higher* rankings.

Likert Rating Scales

Likert scales are probably the best-known rating scales. They are usually characterized by the headings "Strongly Agree," "Agree," "Disagree," and "Strongly Disagree," although the "Strongly Agree" and "Strongly Disagree" headings are optional.

The instructor. . .	Strongly Agree	Agree	Neutral	Disagree	Strongly Disagree
Spoke clearly.	___	___	___	___	___
Graded fairly.	___	___	___	___	___
Discouraged questions.	___	___	___	___	___

Technically, the definition of a Likert scale is somewhat different, but most laypeople think of a Likert scale this way. The comments here on Likert scales also apply to any rating scales with headings that span spectrums from one extreme to the other (e.g., "Very Positive" to "Very Negative," "Very Comfortable" to "Very Uncomfortable," "Strongly Approve" to "Strongly Disapprove," "Much Better" to "Much Worse").

Advantages. Many people are familiar with Likert scales and therefore find them easy to complete. Like other rating scales, Likert scales are efficient (a great deal of information can be provided quickly and compactly) and permit comparisons among answers within the scale. Likert scales are more successfully used to measure attitudes or opinions rather than factual information.

Disadvantages. Novice researchers are often tempted to construct an entire questionnaire of Likert items to facilitate data analysis. Don't do this if it means forcing some items into an inappropriate, awkward, or unclear format.

It is often difficult to write unambiguous items for Likert scales. Think of the very different people who might agree with "I seldom attend parties" or disagree with "My math course requires about as much time and effort as other courses."

Because people are generally more inclined to agree than disagree with a statement, Likert scale items may yield biased results. For more discussion of this problem and how to avoid it, see the discussions on validity and preventing bias in Chapter 3.

What is a "yeasayer/naysayer effect"? Some people with generally positive feelings toward a subject will check all the "Strongly Agree" responses without reading the individual items. Likewise, some people with generally negative feelings will check all the "Strongly Disagree" responses without reading the items. This is called the "yeasayer/naysayer" effect. To prevent it, keep at least some of your statements negative or presenting an opposing view.

Using a "Neutral" or "Don't know" response. Should you put a "Neutral" or "Neither Agree Nor Disagree" column in the center of your Likert scale? It depends on whether it's appropriate to force your respondents to agree or disagree. Suppose you are surveying students on whether "The instructor spoke clearly." It could be argued that the instructor either spoke clearly or didn't, and every student should be able to either agree or disagree with that statement. But on other questions, such as "The President is doing a good job," it could be argued that some people might be truly neutral on this issue.

Should you force an opinion at all? Use of a "Not Sure," "Undecided," "No Opinion," or "Don't Know" column is optional, depending on whether you want to force an opinion. If you decide to leave out this choice and force an opinion, you may be forcing a lie from someone unfamiliar with the issue. But if you include it, some people will use it as a way out of expressing opinions they'd prefer not to take the time to think out. And you won't be able to tell (without further questions) whether an "Undecided" respondent is truly that or really "Uninformed." The decision depends on your questions and the people you are surveying.

Note that "Don't Know" is very different from a "Neutral" opinion. A "Neutral" column should be placed in the center of your Likert scale and included in your data analysis. A "Don't Know" response, however, amounts to someone refusing to answer the question. "Don't Know" responses should be treated as missing data in your data analysis.

I should point out that not all researchers agree with these approaches. Some argue that "Neutral" and "Don't Know" mean the same thing. Rensis Likert, in his original proposal for a Likert scale back in 1932, proposed five categories: strongly approve, approve, undecided, disapprove, and strongly disapprove. One could argue, with some validity, who am I to disagree with the originator of the Likert scale!

How to analyze responses. The appropriate way to analyze Likert scales is a hotly disputed issue within the general field of social science research. Some researchers point out that the data yield ordered but not scaled data (because we cannot be sure that the degree of difference between "Strongly Agree" and "Agree" is the same as the difference between "Agree" and "Neutral"). They therefore argue that Likert data should be analyzed using only non-parametric statistics for ordered data (these are described in Chapter 6).

Others, however, argue that many parametric data analyses for scaled data are sufficiently "robust" to be used with Likert data. ("Robust" means that, while these statistical analyses assume that the data are scaled, using interval data will probably not change the results significantly.) These researchers point to the multitude of published journal articles using such analysis with these kinds of data as evidence that this approach is widely accepted. The references on statistical analysis in the "For More Information" section at the back of this book include a number of citations supporting this stance. Taking this view opens a world of possible statistical analyses.

So which approach should you take? I opt for the latter approach, because (1) there *is* a lot in the literature to support this approach, and (2) your readers are much more likely to be familiar with parametric than non-parametric analyses (t-tests vs. Mann-Whitney U tests, for example), so your findings will be easier to communicate. If you suspect that someone will challenge you on your analysis choice, do both analyses—parametric and non-parametric. If you get the same results for both, go ahead and report the parametric results with a clear conscience. If the results differ, you may wish to report the non-parametric results instead.

Given all this, how should you analyze Likert scale data? It's easiest if you first assign code numbers to each response category. You could code "Strong Agree" as 5, "Agree" as 4, etc.

If you simply want to *describe* your results, use your codes to compute either a mean or median rating, depending on which of the two approaches discussed above you decide on. It can sometimes also be helpful to compute some measure of how spread out the responses are; this shows whether respondents had similar or widely varying opinions. Compute either a standard deviation or semi-interquartile range to show this measure.

If you want to see if the ratings of a set of Likert items differ significantly from one another, use a one-way analysis of variance or a Friedman two-way analysis of variance. If you are comfortable using parametric statistics with Likert scale data, the responses to these items can be incorporated into many other analyses, including multiple analysis of variance, regression and factor analysis.

How to report results. Probably the simplest way to report the results of a Likert scale is to type onto a copy of the questionnaire the percent of respondents choosing each response category. (Be sure to round your percents to two places.) Alternatively, you could prepare a bar graph for each item, with one bar for each response category. This is probably more information, however, than your readers need. You may want to include this kind of detail only for certain items of particular interest.

You can also report mean or median ratings for each item; just be sure to explain your coding scheme to your readers. You may also want to report standard deviations if they help make an important point. To compare responses among a number of Likert scale items, use a bar graph showing the mean or median rating of each item. (If the items are more than a word or two, use horizontal bars so the text of each item can be easily shown.) Alternatively, you can type an "X" or other symbol on a copy of the questionnaire at each item's median point.

Semantic Differential Rating Scales

Another special kind of rating scale is the semantic differential. It consists of antonyms with anywhere from four to seven spaces in between. The respondent marks the space in the item below that best reflects his or her opinion:

> The library's services are:
>
> | | | | | | | |
> |---|---|---|---|---|---|---|
> | Useful | ___ | ___ | ___ | ___ | ___ | Useless |
> | Slow | ___ | ___ | ___ | ___ | ___ | Fast |
> | For Faculty | ___ | ___ | ___ | ___ | ___ | For Students |

Advantages. Like the Likert scale, semantic differentials are an efficient way to collect a great deal of information, and they make straightforward comparisons among answers.

Disadvantages. It is often difficult to give concise written directions for semantic differentials, especially to respondents unfamiliar with this kind of rating scale.

Semantic differential items can only be used when you have obvious antonyms for the subject at hand, and they easily slip into trivia. One might be tempted to ask, for example, if the athletic facilities are useful/useless, adequate/inadequate, well designed/poorly designed, and convenient/inconvenient, when any one of these pairs might be adequate.

Tips on writing. As with Likert scales, avoid a "yeasayer/naysayer effect" by putting some negative words or phrases on the left side as well as the right. Five spaces between antonyms are usually adequate for most purposes. More spaces can increase explained variance, but people cannot distinguish well among more than seven.

How to analyze responses and report results. See the comments above on analyzing and reporting Likert scale data; they apply to semantic differentials as well.

Ecosystem Rating Scales

Webster's defines an ecosystem as "the complex of a community and its environment functioning as an ecological unit in nature." An ecosystem rating scale (also known as goal attainment scaling or GAS or gap analysis) asks for two ratings, with the second rating giving information on the environment in which the first rating was made. The second rating thus facilitates interpretation of the first by helping us understand the "complex" of the initial rating and its environment.

Ecosystems are most commonly used in evaluation studies to measure the attainment of goals and objectives. They usually consist of a set of goal statements. The respondent is asked to rate each statement (usually on a 1 to 5 scale) *twice*, first on the growth *obtained* and second on the growth *desired*, as shown here:

	Growth obtained	Growth desired
An appreciation of the limitations of our current knowledge.	—	—
An understanding of the nature of science and scientific research.	—	—
Awareness of the value of pursuing lifelong education.	—	—

Responses in the second column greatly improve interpretation of the first. If a statement receives a low "growth obtained" rating, for example, the "growth desired" rating will tell you whether you indeed have a problem.

The ecosystem concept can be used to help interpret many other types of ratings or evaluations. The first rating might ask for the respondent's satisfaction with a service, for example. The second rating could then ask for the relative importance or value of that service, how frequently the respondent uses the service, or how much improvement the respondent has seen in the service over the last year. Appendix 3 presents several rating scales using an ecosystem format.

Advantages. Because of its dual-rating approach, an ecosystem is probably one of the best means available to measure the attainment of goals and objectives. The ecosystem is efficient, and its second rating greatly facilitates interpretation of your findings and makes comparisons easy. Consider one of the items in the example above: "An understanding of the nature of science and scientific research." If you only asked for a rating of "Growth obtained," and most respondents gave it a "3," you would probably be concerned. But suppose most respondents gave "Growth desired" a rating of "2." That shows they grew more in this regard than they had wanted to—a positive outcome!

Disadvantages. The chief disadvantage of an ecosystem rating scale is that it is difficult to provide concise, clearly written directions for it. Some people may find ecosystems difficult, frustrating, or time-consuming to complete. Since you are asking for two ratings rather than one, an ecosystem will take respondents considerably longer to complete than other rating scales. And the second rating often requires people to *think* and reflect—more so than do many other survey items.

Tips on writing. The trick to writing an ecosystem rating scale is to have good, clear directions. Describe the meaning of each 5-to-1 rating number (e.g., excellent, good, etc.). Give the most positive rating the highest rating number.

How to analyze responses. As with other rating scales, social scientists disagree on whether parametric statistics for scaled data are appropriate for ecosystems. (See the section on Likert scales above for a full discussion of this issue.)

If you simply want to *describe* your results, compute a mean or median for each rating. It can sometimes be helpful to compute some measure of how spread out the responses are; this shows whether respondents had similar or widely varying opinions. Compute either a standard deviation or semi-interquartile range to show this.

Because one of the reasons you are using an ecosystem is to compare two ratings for each item, you should also compute the difference for each pair of means or medians. To see if the difference is statistically significantly different from zero, test the difference between the two means using a t-test for matched pairs.

If you want to compare the ratings in just one column to see if they differ significantly from one another, use a one-way analysis of variance or a Friedman two-way analysis of variance. If you are comfortable using parametric statistics with rating scale data, the responses to these items can be incorporated into many other analyses, including multiple analysis of variance, regression and factor analysis.

How to report results. Many of the earlier comments on analyzing and reporting Likert scale data also apply to ecosystems. Probably the simplest way to report the results of an ecosystem is to type onto a copy of the questionnaire the mean or median ratings for each item, adding a third column showing the difference between the two. You should indicate which differences are significantly different from zero.

Because there are three important figures associated with each ecosystem item (the two rating means and their difference), ecosystems usually yield too many numbers to be presented in a simple graph. Appendix 7 gives some examples of simple tables that present ecosystem results effectively.

Other Rating Scales

You can make up your own rating scale. Many people use "Excellent, good, fair, poor" or "Frequently, sometimes, never." The letter grades A, B, C, D, and E are an excellent choice when asking for evaluations because they are universally understood and yield scaled data.

Advantages. Any rating scale in a grid format is *efficient:* respondents can give you a tremendous amount of information quickly and easily. Rating scales also let you compare responses among various questions. Making up your own rating scale is the appropriate choice when none of the other formats described in this chapter appear to fit your needs.

Disadvantages. When you depart from accepted formats, you run the increased risk that respondents may be confused by an unfamiliar rating scale. It is even more important than usual that you pilot-test your questionnaire carefully before administering it.

Tips on writing. The general principles used to construct other rating scales apply to your own as well.

Whenever you use a rating scale with a grid format, label *each column* with names, not just numbers. Don't ask, for example, for a rating of 1 through 5, with 1 being "most" and 5 being "least." People will have different concepts of 2, 3, and 4 unless you spell them out. Do you want 3 to mean "usual" or "expected average," for example?

Some people find it hard to squeeze the headings into the columns of a Likert scale, and instead head them with numbers, providing a key that explains the numbers. This is always more confusing and frustrating for your respondents than a descriptive heading and should be avoided if possible. If you can't avoid it, remember that people instinctively associate higher numbers with more positive attributes (they remember from school days that 100 points is an A, while 0 is an F), so assign the highest numbers to the positive side of the scale.

Provide definitions of your terms if there is any chance they will be misinterpreted. If you use a letter-grade rating scale, for example, keep in mind that some people consider C average while others consider it below average. People will also have different definitions of terms like "satisfactory" and "often" unless you provide a definition.

Be careful to mix positive and negative statements, if possible, to avoid a possible "yeasayer/naysayer" effect.

Don't use more than four or five columns if possible—certainly no more than seven. People tend to shy away from extreme categories and stay in the middle.

How to analyze responses and report results. See the comments above on analyzing and reporting Likert scale data; they apply to most rating scales whose responses fall into a meaningful continuum. If your grid asks respondents to choose among categories such as "Helpful, knowledgeable, courteous, efficient," which don't fall into any continuum, you don't have a rating scale. Instead, you have a series of multiple-choice questions with identical options. See the section on multiple-choice questions for suggestions for analyzing and reporting such data.

Open-Ended Questions

Open-ended or free-response questions leave a blank space where the respondent composes his or her own answer as in this example:

What was the *one best* part of this program?

_____

Sentence completion items like the one below are a special kind of open-ended question:

More than anything else, I would advise new freshmen to

_____.

Advantages. There are four occasions when open-ended items may be best:

1.   When many answers (more than six or seven) are possible, or when a multiple-choice question might overlook some important responses.

2.   When you are asking for occupation.

3.   When a multiple-choice item might bias responses by steering respondents in a particular direction.

4.   When your question is interesting enough that people will *want* to answer it. People enjoy being asked, "How would you improve . . . ?", for example.

Open-ended questions are also useful in pilot studies for drafting more specific questions for the final study. The most common responses can become the choices in a multiple-choice question.

Disadvantages. Open-ended questions are not very popular with respondents, since they make them work harder and lengthen the time required to complete the questionnaire. Very often the respondent will leave them blank, along with the rest of the questionnaire!

Open-ended questions are not very popular with researchers, either, since the answers are generally difficult to read, categorize, process, and interpret. The data must be analyzed subjectively, not objectively.

Because of these disadvantages, open-ended questions should be used sparingly in any questionnaire. If you find your questionnaire is largely comprised of open-ended questions, consider switching to a telephone survey or focus groups.

Tips on writing. The amount of space allotted for an open-ended item should give a clue to the expected response length. Keep it as short as possible, and rule the space to make answers easier to write and read.

Sentence completion items will be most successful if they ask for a response of just a word or two and if the blank is at the *end* of the sentence.

How to analyze responses. The major problem with open-ended questions is figuring out how to analyze the answers. Fortunately, software to help with this task (called qualitative data analysis) is increasingly available. Coding responses to open-ended questions is discussed in Chapter 5, and references on qualitative data analyses and software are given in the "For More Information" section at the end of this book.

How to report results. Open-ended questions are most commonly reported by stating the percentage of respondents giving each of the most common responses. If you ask students to "Name *one* thing about Baldwin College that *most* needs improvement," for example, you might report that 15% mentioned registration, 12% mentioned the food, 9% mentioned the social life, and 14% mentioned something else, with 50% not mentioning anything. A few quotations from open-ended questions can add "sparkle" and credibility to your report and help readers who are uncomfortable with numbers understand your results.

In some evaluation studies, the people in charge of the program under evaluation will want to see *all* open-ended responses verbatim. This is feasible only with relatively small-scale surveys (an evaluation of a small conference, for example).

In these cases, have all the responses to each open-ended item typed up together, so readers can scan the list and see for themselves what the most frequent comments were to that question. If you think it would be helpful, group similar comments together and give them simple headings ("Comments about registration").

Chapter 3

Developing the Survey Instrument

Now that we have discussed planning your survey and the kind of questionnaire items you might employ, you're ready to draft the questionnaire. This chapter will discuss drafting individual items and assembling them into a questionnaire.

What Goes into a Good Questionnaire Item?

The fundamental characteristic of a good questionnaire item is that it is *clearly understood*. When respondents find your question difficult to understand or answer, he or she is likely to mentally change it in some way that makes it easier to answer. Respondents may answer what they think is the "spirit" of the question rather than the actual question itself. We don't want our respondents doing this; we want them answering *our* questions, not theirs.

Using the following methods, you can ensure your question will be clear to your respondents, so they will all interpret it in the same way:

Keep it short. Short, straightforward items are easier to understand than compound or complex statements and therefore yield more accurate answers. They also mean a shorter questionnaire and therefore an increased response rate. Lengthy questions may cause the respondent to lose focus and may also cause fatigue and impatience.

Here is an example of a question that could be made much shorter:

> Which of the following statements best describes your enrollment pattern at Briggs College?
> ____ I was enrolled primarily as a full-time student.
> ____ I was enrolled primarily as a part-time student.

Rewrite each question several times, trying to simplify each sentence as much as possible.

Make sure it asks only one question. Rather than ask, "Should 18-year olds have the rights of an adult?", specify which rights you mean: voting, drinking, marriage, or whatever. A "double-barreled" item like the following asks several questions that might each be answered differently: "Do you feel that computer literacy is, or should be, an objective or requirement of the college?" "Is this job a step toward your career goals or related to your major?" To avoid this problem, check your use of the words "and" and "or" and limit your questions to *one* adjective or adverb each.

Keep it readable. Keep the vocabulary level low; go over each word in your item and make sure it is as simple as possible. Avoid the jargon of your field; don't use words like "attrition," "personnel," "networking," or "articulation," for example. Here's an item that's loaded with jargon:

> Please indicate yes or no in each of the following cases in which you *use* computing services.
>
> 1 Data Base Management
> 2 Word Processing
> 3 Record Keeping
> 4 Spreadsheet Analysis
> 5 Data Analysis and/or Research
> 6 Programming

I learned through a pilot study that the following item also has jargon.

> Are you primarily interested in taking courses for credit, or would you prefer to attend non-credit courses?
> ___ Credit
> ___ Non-credit

"Credit" and "non-credit" may be incomprehensible to people who have never gone to college.

Avoid negative items. If you must have them, underline them and/or put them in all capital letters or boldface to draw attention to them: <u>*NOT*</u>, <u>***EXCEPT***</u>, etc. Beware of double negatives and other easily confused phrases. Also avoid words which mean different things to different people.

Make all definitions, assumptions, and qualifiers clearly understood. Clarify terms that could be misunderstood. A question like "Do you use the IBM mainframe computer?" can be interpreted many ways. One person could say that anyone who's ever looked at a printout is technically a user; another could say that only those with "hands on" experience are users. Similarly, rather than asking for age, ask for year of birth or age as of January 1. Terms like "adequate," "minority," "value," "how much," "usually," "access," "convenient," "most," "quality," "procedures," "diversity," "not too often," "acceptable," "very often," and "now" are full of ambiguities. Even seemingly straightforward words like "you" and "never" can be misinterpreted (Is "you" singular or plural? Does "never" mean "absolutely never" or "virtually never"?).

When asking for an estimate of something, spell out the period of time you are interested in: last week? per day? When you ask for salary, similarly specify whether you want gross or net salary and whether you want salary rate per year, per month, biweekly, weekly, or per hour. In fact, specify the unit of measurement for *all* numerical responses. Do you want the student's course load expressed as number of courses or number of credits? Label the response blank with the appropriate unit of measurement to help clarify your question.

When asking for a rating or comparison, make sure you give a clear point of reference. Spell out the criteria to be used. Do you want the staff rated on courtesy, cheerfulness, helpfulness, or knowledge? Is an "above average" response in terms of actual or desired performance? In terms of employees here or employees in general?

If your question includes a qualifying phrase (e.g., "except for housing," "if you commute"), place it at the beginning of your stem. Your sentence structure may not be the best, but the qualifier won't be overlooked.

Make sure your questions have no hidden assumptions written into them. How many assumptions can you find in this classic: "Have you stopped beating your wife?"

When it comes to definitions, assumptions, and qualifiers, consider the feelings of your respondent. Don't phrase definitions in such a way that he or she feels stupid. Make sure the respondent has all the information necessary to answer the question. Be careful of presuming, say, that the respondent has graduated from high school.

Avoid making significant memory demands. Don't ask alumni, for example, how they felt about your institution as freshmen. You can't possibly get accurate answers; too much has happened to your respondents between then and now that will color their memories. Asking, "How many times did you visit the library last week?" will give you more valid data than asking, "How many times did you visit the library last year?"

Consider this question:

How much do you usually spend on textbooks each semester?

This item requires the respondent to recall and make a mental average of spending over several semesters. The question would be greatly improved if it were rewritten as:

About how much did you spend on textbooks last fall?

It's more likely that your respondents could answer this question more accurately because its memory and cognitive demands are not as great.

Avoid asking for very precise responses. Questions asking for a very precise response (such as annual salary to the exact dollar, grade point average to two decimal places, how many times the respondent visited the library or called home in the past year) make severe memory cognitive demands on respondents and will not be answered accurately. Rather than asking for an exact amount, use a multiple-choice or rating scale format.

Respondents will also respond less accurately to a question with many response categories (for instance, a question asking the respondent to identify which one of ten listed factors was most important in deciding to attend your school), than a question with just a couple of response categories.

Avoid asking for broad generalizations about attitudes or opinions. It is harder for people to make broad generalizations, especially about their feelings or opinions, than to describe concrete actions. Opinion questions are also often harder to analyze and interpret than behavioral "vignette" questions, since respondents' views come from different frames of reference. Student opinions of your advisement program, for example, may be based in part on the quality of their high school advisement experiences, the experiences of their friends, or on stories they've heard about advisement at other colleges.

Your questionnaire will therefore be less ambiguous and more reliable if you make as many items as possible concrete or "behavioral": asking for a behavior rather than a feeling or opinion. For example, instead of asking, "Do you consider yourself a hardworking student?," ask, "How many hours per day do you usually study?" or "How many hours did you study yesterday?" Try asking several questions and inferring an opinion rather than simply asking for the opinion.

Don't try to make your questions *too* specific, however. A large number of "trivial" questions may cause confusion or a loss of interest and will lengthen your questionnaire considerably.

Make the item easy and fast to answer. The respondent should easily understand how to decide on an answer and how to record it. A simple answer format requiring only a few checks is better than a complicated scoring key.

Keep it interesting. Don't let your items get pedestrian or monotonous. The six items below would quickly frustrate almost any respondent:

How important is your need to locate information of the following types?

	Least important				Most important
Simple facts for course purposes	___	___	___	___	___
Simple facts for research purposes	___	___	___	___	___
Simple facts for general purposes	___	___	___	___	___
Complex data for course purposes	___	___	___	___	___
Complex data for research purposes	___	___	___	___	___
Complex data for general purposes	___	___	___	___	___

Many people write questionnaires using the same kind of item format (e.g., a Likert scale) throughout. While this makes it very easy to compare responses to different items, it can also make the questionnaire monotonous and boring. Try to use a variety of formats, although not so many that your respondents might get confused.

Avoid biased, loaded, leading, or sensitive questions. While no ethical researcher writes these kinds of questions on purpose, it's easy to write them inadvertently. Here are some examples (all from real surveys!):

> Do you agree that computer literacy should be an objective or requirement of the college?

> Are you concerned that higher education spending is rising faster than health-care spending?

> Do you favor requiring full-time professors at institutions which receive state funds to spend a minimum number of hours teaching?

> Should travel costs ($76 million) for faculty members at public institutions in our state be sharply reduced?

> Should harsher penalties be enacted for crimes committed against the elderly?

> Do you feel there is too much power concentrated in the hands of labor union officials?

> Are you in favor of forcing state, county, and municipal employees to pay union dues to hold their government jobs?

These questions are biased because they are all presented as statements that respondents must agree or disagree with, and respondents generally find it easier and less threatening to agree than disagree. They are also "loaded" with non-neutral terms, such as "harsher," "power" and "forcing." Furthermore, the questions present arguments on only one side of the issue; as many of the questions now stand, few would disagree with them.

To avoid biased, leading, or loaded questions, try the following:

*   ***Imagine you're writing questions from the opposite point of view.*** For example, if you're trying to collect data to support the need for expanded counseling services, imagine you're trying to cut back on them. Would you still ask the same questions and phrase them the same way?

- ***Ask about both the pros and cons of an issue.*** Don't ask the respondent to make criticisms without giving him or her a chance to praise as well. And don't ask the respondent if he or she is in favor of a new program or extending the hours that an office is open (who wouldn't be?) without noting the costs and liabilities.

- ***Avoid questions that people are uncomfortable answering honestly.*** People tend to be comfortable with the status quo, to deceive themselves as well as others about their propensities in sensitive areas, and to be reluctant to admit any inferiority or wrongdoing. Many will not answer honestly if you ask them whether they smoke, watch TV, go to art museums or church, or vote. Many will also not report accurately their salary, their age, their job, their grade point average, whether they failed a particular course, and whether they were rejected from other schools to which they applied. (In a December 1963 survey, 63 percent of respondents said they voted for Kennedy in 1960. In reality, he won with less than 51 percent of the vote.) Many people will indicate they agree with the statement, "I believe all people should be respected as equals," even if they demonstrate prejudice or intolerance toward certain groups.

  Be very careful phrasing any questions whose responses have any potential level of social desirability. In some instances, such as asking about age or salary, people may respond more truthfully to broad categories than a request for a specific figure.

  Questions worded in the first person ("Do you cheat?") will be answered differently from those in the third person ("Do your friends cheat?"). Some respondents may find third-person questions easier to answer honestly.

  Try not to phrase questions in a psychologically threatening way. Rather than ask *if* a respondent does something good or bad (e.g., vote, cheat on tests), ask how *often* he or she does it. It also helps to ask about very specific behaviors. If you ask, "Did you glance at your neighbor's paper during the last math test?", some respondents may not even realize you are asking about cheating behavior. Others may recognize your intent but still feel they can answer your question honestly without labeling themselves "cheaters."

Bottom line: Few researchers have the skill to conduct the level of research needed to elicit accurate answers to sensitive questions. If you're not confident you'll get an accurate, honest answer, don't ask the question.

- *If appropriate, let people admit they don't know or can't remember.* Forcing an opinion from people who don't have one or a memory from people who can't remember one is tantamount to forcing them to lie. Consider, for example, the following statement: "Bradham College's administrators talk about the importance of diversity, but I never see them attending diversity programs." Students who do not attend diversity programs themselves, or who do not know many administrators, cannot respond validly to this statement.

- *Use two different versions of the question in two different parts of the questionnaire.* Do this in your pilot test and see how the responses differ, then decide which one(s) to use in the final version.

- *Use multiple assessments with a variety of methods, formats, and topics*. The only way you can be sure your questions aren't biased or leading is to cross-check your responses against other data. This concept is called "triangulation" and we'll discuss it in the following sections.

Should You Be Concerned about the Validity and Reliability of Your Questionnaire?

This depends on the subject and purpose of your study. A simple, straightforward "one shot" study on a non-controversial subject, whose results are only for general information and not for a specific decision, probably doesn't need much evidence of reliability or validity. You should consider collecting evidence of reliability and validity, however, if your study has any of the following characteristics:

- Your findings may lead to major changes.

- The study concerns a controversial subject and the findings may be hotly disputed.

- The study concerns a sensitive issue on which respondents may not answer truthfully.

- There is disagreement about the definitions or assumptions you are building into your study (e.g., Do all students need an academic advisor? What constitutes advisement?).

- The study is part of a substantial, expensive, perhaps longitudinal research project.

Be aware, however, that even a simple, seemingly straightforward survey may generate erroneous responses and could therefore benefit from some evidence of reliability and validity. Respondents may not recall accurately even simple facts, such as whether your school was their first choice or to which other schools they applied. If they cannot recall these simple matters accurately, they will probably be even more inaccurate when asked for an attitude, an opinion, or an assessment or when asked any question that makes complex memory demands or other cognitive demands. It's therefore always prudent to consider collecting some evidence of reliability and validity. Of the two, validity is far more important than reliability (collecting reliability evidence alone may only demonstrate that your data are reliably, consistently worthless!).

What is Reliability?

A *reliable* questionnaire elicits *consistent* responses. An absolutely, perfectly reliable questionnaire is impossible to create, however. Why? There are many, many reasons why a person's response might vary from one question to the next or from one survey to the next. Many of these factors are beyond our control, for example:

- Variations in mood

- Fluctuations and idiosyncrasies of human memory

- Unpredictable fluctuations in attention or accuracy

- Health

- Fatigue

- Room conditions such as heat, light, noise (You can control these conditions to some extent in an in-person administration but not in a mailed or telephone survey.)

- Momentary distractions

- Group homogeneity (Other things being equal, the responses of a group that all feels pretty much the same about your issue will have weaker reliability evidence than a group with widely divergent opinions.)

To get an idea of how much these factors contribute to inconsistent answers, imagine throwing a softball or rolling a bowling ball over and over again. Most of us will not consistently throw or roll the ball as far or to exactly the same spot. If we can't control our body movements consistently, how can we possibly do so with our brains? For this reason, there will always be some inconsistency in your respondents' answers, no matter how good your survey is.

There are other factors, however, over which we may have some control.

- Inaccuracies in scoring, especially open-ended questions

- Motivation

- Familiarity and comfort with the item formats we are using

- The order in which questions are asked

- How clear the directions are

- How clear the questions are: Will they be interpreted by everyone in the same way?

- How long the questionnaire is (Other things being equal, a long questionnaire will be more reliable than a short one.)

While we can never have a perfectly reliable survey, we can certainly do all we can to control these factors and make our surveys as reliable as possible.

- We can establish controlled, double-checked practices to ensure that scoring is consistent and accurate.

- Through an effective cover letter, we can do all we can to motivate the respondent to give full attention to the survey.

- We can use simple item formats with clear directions, so everyone understands them and understands them consistently.

- We can ask the questions in a consistent order from one survey to the next.

- We can do our utmost to write clear questions that will be understood consistently by everyone.

- We can make the survey long enough to enhance its reliability, if that is important to us.

What Kinds of Reliability or Consistency Can You Assess?

There are two kinds of consistency that we can look for in a questionnaire:

Consistency within the questionnaire. (This is called internal consistency.) Responses to similar questions within a questionnaire should be similar. You can identify inconsistent responses by putting two very similar questions in different parts of the questionnaire and seeing if the responses are similar. If a respondent says she likes your institution at the beginning of the questionnaire, for example, a similar question at the end of the survey should get a similar response. You would also expect at least moderate agreement among a group of items all asking about math anxiety.

This kind of reliability is most relevant if the survey focuses on just one consistent issue, such as satisfaction with your institution, indicators of dropping out before graduating, satisfaction with a course or instructor, or attitudes toward diversity. Unfortunately, many questionnaires ask a variety of questions about a variety of topics, so it is difficult to measure their internal consistency. To do so, you must ask at least two questions on the same subject, and to keep the questionnaire as short as possible we often ask only one question on each topic.

If you wish to demonstrate the internal consistency of your survey, how can you balance the need to, in essence, ask each question twice with the need for a short survey? It is the rare survey that has such a compelling need for documented internal consistency that each subject must be addressed twice. Try reframing just a couple of the most important questions. Try also comparing answers to questions that are similar but not identical (for example, questions on attitudes toward different racial/ethnic groups).

Consistency over time. (This is called test-retest reliability.) Questionnaire responses should be consistent over time. If an alum says he likes your institution, he should say he likes your institution a week later, a month later, or a year later (assuming nothing as happened in the interim to change his mind.)

Unfortunately, questionnaire surveys often measure volatile opinions. Over time, many people will change their attitudes and opinions about your institution, its programs and faculty, and various issues of the day. Their plans, goals, and values may change as well. In these cases, this kind of reliability may be irrelevant.

Consistency over time is only a rare concern since most questionnaires deal with opinions or other information that is expected to change over time. Indeed, the purpose of a questionnaire study is often to collect information to help us facilitate change.

How is Reliability Established?

The fundamental way to measure reliability is through correlations of individual items or overall questionnaire "scores." Here is another problem with assessing questionnaire reliability: it cannot be done with nominal data, such as that from a multiple-choice item, because correlations cannot be computed for such data. If your questionnaire consists of scaled or "interval" items, here is how to measure its reliability:

Internal consistency is measured by correlating item scores with one another in some fashion, generally using a statistic called a correlation. There are a number of formulas for doing this, including split-half reliabilities, the Spearman-Brown prophesy formula, Kuder-Richardson formula 20 (KR 20), KR 21, coefficient alpha, and discrimination indices. For information on how to compute any of these, see the references in the "For More Information" section at the end of this book.

Test-retest reliability is measured by administering an identical questionnaire at a later date to the same sample of people and correlating their responses to the two questionnaires.

What is Validity?

Unlike reliability, validity does not have an obvious synonym, so it is harder to define and explain. The closest synonym I can come up with is *truthfulness*: if a questionnaire is valid, you are finding out what respondents *really, truthfully* think about what you *really, truthfully* want to know. A *valid* questionnaire, therefore, measures accurately what you want it to measure, and the inferences you make from this questionnaire will be accurate.

Just as we cannot create an absolutely, perfectly reliable questionnaire, neither can we create an absolutely, perfectly valid one. Why? There is no way that we can get inside peoples' minds to find out what they are really, truly thinking. We instead make inferences from the questions we ask and the answers they give, which may not match what's going on inside respondents' heads:

- The questions we pose in our survey may not really, truly match what we want to know, and the person we are surveying cannot get inside our heads to check.

- Even if we've posed our questions accurately, our respondent may misinterpret them, and there is no way we can get inside his or her head to check.

- The answers the respondent gives may not really, truly match what he or she thinks, and again there is no way we can get inside his or her head to check.

- We may misinterpret the respondent's answers and, again, there is no way we can get inside his or her head to check, nor can the respondent get into our heads and check our interpretation.

The extent of a questionnaire's validity also depends on your *use* of it. Student evaluations of courses might, for example, be a useful tool in evaluating curricula but would be invalid for predicting participation in intercollegiate sports. A survey of freshman attitudes toward college might be useful in planning freshman orientation programs but would be invalid for placing freshmen into appropriate math courses. Researchers are increasingly saying that we validate not the questionnaire itself but our *interpretation and use* of its results.

How is Validity Established?

Unlike reliability, which can often be established with a single statistical measure, there is no one measure that is definitive proof of validity. Each measure has inherent inadequacies. "The more, the better" is therefore the rule in establishing evidence of validity. Because we cannot "get inside peoples' heads," validity is established through *corroborating evidence*. The more corroborating measures you collect, and the more disparate they are in nature, the better your evidence that your questionnaire is valid.

There are four basic ways that survey researchers can develop evidence of validity:

1. Compare or correlate survey results with results from a variety of other measures and data collection methods. You could, for example,

   o compare results of a survey designed to predict student attrition with later actual attrition;

   o compare survey results with results of telephone interviews with a sample of respondents;

   o compare survey results with results of focus groups on the same topic;

o   compare results of a survey of student attitudes toward mathematics (e.g., "mathophobia") with faculty ratings of those students' attitudes toward mathematics; and

o   compare results of a survey of study habits and attitudes with grades.

The process of using multiple measures and multiple methods, correlating everything, and seeing if the correlations make sense is sometimes called *triangulation*. As you plan your validation measures, include some correlations that should be comparatively low. Your survey results should probably have fairly low correlations, for example, with color preference, month of birth, or knowledge of skiing techniques.

This kind of evidence can be difficult to establish if either the questionnaire or the "other measures" have categorical data, such as those from a multiple-choice item, because traditional correlations cannot be computed for such data. This kind of evidence is easiest to collect when all your questionnaire items focus on one topic (e.g., intent to drop out, attitudes toward diversity) and a total "score" can be computed.

2.   Compare results from diverse groups to see if the differences match what others have found. For example,

o   Do the results for traditionally-aged and non-traditionally-aged students differ as one would expect?

o   Are alumni who are satisfied with their institution more likely to make financial contributions to it than alumni who are dissatisfied? You could validate an alumni satisfaction survey by comparing the results with alumni giving.

o   Do students who are satisfied with a faculty member earn higher grades than those who are dissatisfied? You could validate a student course evaluation survey by comparing the results with final grades.

o   Are students who profess greater tolerance for diversity more likely to join groups with diverse membership, attend lectures by diverse speakers, or elect courses with diverse content? You could validate a survey of student attitudes toward diversity by comparing the results with participation in these activities.

o   College men generally rate themselves higher in leadership skills than college women. You could validate a survey of student leadership skills and attitudes by comparing the results for men and women.

3.   Have people with diverse backgrounds and viewpoints review the survey before it is administered. Find out if

o   each item is clear and easily understood,

o   they interpret each item in the intended way,

o   the items have an intuitive relationship to the study's topic and goals, and

o   your intent behind each item is clear to colleagues knowledgeable about the subject..

4.   Pilot test the survey. If you are surveying student satisfaction with your college, for example, pilot test it with some students who are both satisfied and dissatisfied with your college. Also pilot test the survey with students from a variety of majors and lifestyles.

The last two methods do not require statistical analysis. They are therefore the least difficult to collect, although they are more subjective and may be more difficult to interpret. These forms of validity evidence should be a key element of any survey study, no matter how mundane.

There are a few additional steps you can take to ensure that your questionnaire's results are valid. Follow all the steps given earlier in this chapter to prepare good questionnaire items, particularly striving to keep them free from bias and ambiguities. If you are concerned that some respondents may not answer your questionnaire truthfully, include a few items solely to check the validity of responses, such as asking respondents if they belong to a nonexistent group. And do all you can to achieve a high response rate, following the tips in Chapter 4.

How Should the Items Be Ordered in the Questionnaire?

The first questions should be chosen with care. They should be questions that will "hook" the respondent into answering the survey and thus increase your response rate. Your first questions should have the following characteristics:

- They should be *intriguing*, the kind of question that makes your respondent think, "I'm glad they asked me that! I've always wanted to tell someone what I thought about that!" Perhaps you could ask for an opinion on an interesting (but relatively benign) topic or for some interesting information on the respondent's background ("Why did you decide to attend this college?"). Demographic questions (e.g., on sex, age, major) should *not* go first.

- They should be *easy to answer*. They should not require a lot of deep thought and should be answerable with a simple check mark. This is not the place to put complicated rating scales or open-ended questions.

- They should be *general*. Most people have an easier time moving from generalities to specifics than the other way around. Check if the first questions will influence later responses. If so, is this what you want?

- They should be somewhat *impersonal*. While you can ask immediately about general opinions or background, save the sensitive questions for later . . . and this includes many demographic questions (on age and income, for example). "Favorable" questions, such as those asking about accomplishments, are good to put first.

The remaining questions should follow a natural flow, both logically and psychologically. . .like a good story. Try to keep questions on a similar topic together, so the respondent can stay on one train of thought. Within each topic, try to begin with general questions and move into specifics. Try also to group items of the same format together. This is especially important if you're using unique item types with complicated directions.

Avoid contingency questions: those where if you check "yes" to one question, you then "GO TO" another set of questions. They're confusing and frustrating and therefore can reduce response rates. It may be easier to have everyone answer all questions and then delete non-applicable answers yourself during your data analysis. If you do have several questions that you'll want only a small group to answer, put them at the end of the questionnaire and tell everyone else to stop before reaching them. Alternatively, you can send this group a separate questionnaire.

Keep in mind that the order of your questions can contribute to bias. If, for example, you first ask respondents some questions about how they're financing their education, their responses may color their response to a later question on whether college costs are too high.

The last questions should be the ones your respondents will be least enthusiastic about answering. We hope that by this time they're "hooked" and won't mind answering these last few questions. If they do decide to skip them, at least you will have already gotten some data! The following four kinds of questions should be as near the end as possible:

1.   *Delicate, intimate, or sensitive questions.* These include questions on age, salary, personal habits and preferences such as how often someone drinks, and opinions on sensitive subjects like abortion.

2.   *Complex questions* that take a long time to read or a lot of thought to answer.

3.   *Open-ended questions* since these take a long time to answer.

4.   *Boring questions, including demographic items.* Make sure you *really* need each piece of demographic information. Your respondents will find them irritants at best and offensive at worst. Try to make clear why you need this information.

What Else Goes into a Questionnaire?

Beside your questions, your questionnaire needs a title, directions, and a closing.

Title and sponsor. You'd be surprised how often these are neglected! They are important tools in convincing your respondent of the professionalism of your study and therefore in increasing your response rate. The title lets the respondent know what is to come and is an important motivating device. Make the title intriguing enough to pique the respondent's interest and help convince him or her to respond. Including the study's sponsor ("Office of Institutional Research, Atlantic State College") gives the questionnaire credibility and legitimacy.

Some people leave the title and sponsor off the questionnaire because they are identified elsewhere—either in a cover letter or by the person administering the survey. Even in these instances, however, it's important to include these things right on the questionnaire. They add a professional touch that will help convince respondents to take your questionnaire seriously.

Directions should make the respondent *want* to answer truthfully. They should be simply phrased and crystal-clear, telling the respondent how to answer each question and how to record his or her answers. Make clear, for example, whether the respondent should pick the *one* best response or as many as apply. Can he or she elaborate on responses? If so, where? Use boldface, capitals, or italics to draw attention to the directions.

Generally speaking, shorter directions are easier to understand, as in the example below:

> *Confusing:* Please mark the number which more accurately reflects your opinion concerning each question listed below. Circling number 1 would indicate excellent and complete agreement, circling number 2 would indicate satisfactory and general agreement, circling number 3 would indicate unsatisfactory and general disagreement, and circling number 4 would indicate poor and total disagreement.

> *Better:* For each statement below, check the box that most accurately shows your agreement. (These directions would be followed by statements with four columns of boxes labeled "Strongly Agree," "Agree," "Disagree," and "Strongly Disagree.")

Directions are simpler when you use as few different response methods as possible. You may want to consider short introductions to each section to explain new response methods and help respondents "shift gears."

Closing. Don't forget to say thank you! Also repeat directions on how to return the questionnaire. A box to check (and space for an address) if the respondent would like a copy of the results is a nice touch.

How Long Should a Questionnaire Be?

In general, the shorter the questionnaire, the less formidable it looks and therefore the higher the response rate. In some instances, the ideal questionnaire may be on a folded double postcard (the respondent replies on one half, detaches it, and drops it in the mail). In many other circumstances, the best questionnaire is on *one piece of paper.*

If your questionnaire draft does not appear to fit onto one piece of paper, here are some ways to make it shorter:

•   Shorten it! Go over the entire questionnaire. Focus only on the essential questions. Eliminate the ones that would be "nice to know" but can't be used to improve programs and services. (If you're not sure, remove it!) Try to delete all unnecessary words and phrases.

•   Reproduce a two-page questionnaire onto the front *and back* of one piece of paper.

•   If the questionnaire won't quite fit onto the front and back of an 8½ by 11 page, use an 8½ by 14 page, or try an 11 by 17 page folded in half to create a four page survey.

•   Break your questions into two or more questionnaires, sending each to a randomly chosen fraction of your sample (if your sample is sufficiently large to do this). Ask everyone the essential questions, but distribute the remaining questions among the questionnaires.

•   Use a smaller type (but not so small that it's hard to read!). Use a 10- or 11-point font instead of 12-point. Use desktop publishing facilities or professionally typeset your questionnaire if you can. If you can't, perhaps you have access to a photocopier that can "shrink" your typewritten page a bit.

• Leave off the cover page. All it does is warn the respondent that a mighty long questionnaire is underneath!

If you've done all this and your survey is still too long, you're probably trying to cover too much ground with one survey. Review the questions posed in Chapter 1 with the people requesting the survey, making sure it is focused on essential issues only. Point out that follow-up surveys can always be done, and they'll probably be of better quality if they're based on the findings from this survey.

What Should You Keep in Mind as You Have the Questionnaire Typed and Duplicated?

A carefully laid-out, grammatically flawless questionnaire looks shorter and more professional, is much easier to complete, and therefore yields a higher response rate and better quality data. Here are some suggestions:

Cleanly format your questionnaire. Putting the text into two columns rather than running it across the page makes the survey easier to read and shorter in appearance.

Use plenty of "white space." Use generous margins and spacing. If your questions fill only three quarters of a page, spread them out.

Use a smaller (10- or 11-point) font. It makes your questionnaire look not only shorter but also more professional.

"Stack" the responses to multiple-choice items vertically. A respondent can find and mark the appropriate response more easily when the choices are listed in a column rather than across one or two lines:

Confusing: ___ Yes   ___ No

Better: ___ Yes
                  ___ No

Responses in one column are also easier for you and your helpers to find and code, and columns of responses create white space that adds eye appeal.

Make spaces for check marks with professionally drawn boxes such as □, brackets such as [ ], parentheses such as ( ), or simply a short line such as __. Typed boxes made with slashes and underscores look terrible and hand-drawn boxes even worse.

Use your word processing or desktop publishing facilities to their fullest extent. Use horizontal lines, for example, to mark different sections of the survey. Use right justification to bring your questions and responses close together.

Proofread your questionnaire carefully *for grammar and spelling*. A single error will detract from the professional appearance of your questionnaire. Ask some laypeople outside your field to read your questionnaire and let you know of any directions, items, or words they find hard to understand.

Have a data entry professional review the questionnaire if you want the responses keyed into a computer directly from the questionnaires.

Reproduce your questionnaire by the best means possible. Offset printing or top-quality photocopying look best and are not too expensive. Dittos, mimeographs, and fuzzy photocopies look antiquated and unprofessional and can be hard to read.

Use quality paper. Subtly colored paper—nothing garish or too bright to be readable—may be a nice touch with some groups.

Appendix 4 gives a few examples of questionnaires that have been used effectively in institutional research surveys.

What Software Support is Available for Preparing Questionnaires?

In the last few years, a number of software packages to create questionnaires have appeared. Some generate custom-made "bubble sheets" in which respondents fill in "bubbles" rather than make check marks on the questionnaire; others are designed so respondents complete the survey directly at a computer terminal. Some packages process and analyze the results as well as generate the questionnaire. Software packages include:

- Bubble Publishing Form Shop for Windows by Scanning Dynamics, Inc. (800-493-9590 or 804-750-1228)

- Design Expert by NCS Education (800-627-1550)

- DesignWorks and FORMPRO by National Computer Systems (NCS) (800-447-3269)

- FLIPS (Form and Label Integrated Printing System) and ScanSurvey by Scantron Corp. (800-421-5066 or 800-722-6876)

- Questar Data Systems (612-688-0089)

- Raosoft SURVEY and SurveyFirst by Raosoft (206-525-4025)

- ScreenSurvey by the National Research Council of Canada in Ottawa

- SURVEY by Qsoft Solutions (800-669-9701)

- SurveyPro 2.0 by Apian Software (800-237-4565 or 415-694-2900)

- TELEform for Windows by Cardiff Software (800-659-8755)

- TrendTrak Research System by TrendTrak (800-242-8022).

Note that the software market changes quickly; some of these may be published by someone else or no longer available by the time you read this.

Every package has its strengths and weaknesses. Before you start shopping for software, know exactly what you want to do with the software and what features are important to you. Also know your hardware requirements; some packages require certain PCs, printers, or scanners. (NCS and Scantron both sell scanners.) Finally, see if you can use the package on a trial basis; some packages do not offer enough flexibility to create an optimally-formatted questionnaire.

Should you use one of these packages? I myself hesitate to do so, for a couple of reasons. First, these packages all limit your possible questionnaire formats. Software that create custom "bubble sheets" are best for multiple-choice questions and simple rating scales like Likert scales. Creating a more complex rating scale like an ecosystem is difficult if not impossible.

My greater concern, however, is that computer-generated questionnaires look impersonal. It's obvious that the responses are going to be scanned or keyed directly into a computer, and this can give some respondents the impression that no one will look at their individual responses (especially to open-ended items) or really care what they have to say.

Computer-generated questionnaires are therefore best under the following circumstances:

•	You are sending out thousands of questionnaires.

•	You are asking for only very impersonal, factual information.

•	The questionnaires may help convince your respondents of the professionalism of your survey.

•	You do not have the support to get the data entered in any other fashion.

Some researchers who don't have access to one of these packages "semi-computerize" their surveys by placing data entry codes on the questionnaires. Again, these look impersonal, giving some respondents the impression that no one will look at (or care about) their individual responses. The codes may also confuse some respondents. I therefore discourage this practice unless absolutely necessary, for reasons similar to those cited above.

Some researchers try to facilitate data entry by distributing a standard "bubble sheet" to respondents along with a questionnaire. Respondents are then asked to code their responses onto the bubble sheet. This approach is generally ill-advised. Because these sheets are usually designed for five-response multiple-choice items, you will usually be limited to that type of question or perhaps a Likert-type scale. Using a separate response sheet is complicated and cumbersome for respondents and runs contrary to the general precept, "Be considerate of your respondents and make their job as easy as possible" (which we will discuss in the next chapter). Some respondents may find the bubble sheet confusing; others may find it off-putting because it reminds them of a test-taking experience. Using these forms with a mailed survey therefore usually results in a very poor response rate. Even using them with an in-person administration may yield poor-quality data.

If custom-survey software is unavailable and entering data is a significant problem for you, try to be creative. I once worked on a survey where I took the questionnaires home at night and transposed the answers onto bubble sheets myself while I listened to the television. It really didn't take long and was much more convenient for my respondents . . . and probably yielded more accurate data.

Chapter 4

Conducting the Survey

Once you have prepared your questionnaire, you are ready to conduct the survey. In this chapter, we will discuss preparing a questionnaire package for a mailed survey, conducting a pilot test, and administering the survey. We will also discuss what tasks can be delegated to others and ways you can use a personal computer to help you . . . along with things to consider if you decide to conduct your survey on person, via telephone, or using focus groups. But first, let's address a question that's probably uppermost on your mind:

What is an Acceptable Response Rate?

One of the most common questions asked by novice researchers is, "What percentage of my questionnaires do I need to get back?" There are both simple and complex answers to this question. The simple answer is that most pros suggest a 70% to 80% response rate and consider 50% minimally adequate. (True professional survey researchers get well over 95%.)

The complex answer is that this is almost an irrelevant question for two reasons. The first reason is that, as any good researcher will tell you, *quality* of responses is more important than *quantity*. It is more important to have respondents who are representative of the group from which you are sampling than to have a large return rate.

Here's an example. Let's say you are conducting two surveys of your school's student body. Survey #1 yields only a 45% response rate, but the respondents match the student body in terms of proportions of freshmen, sophomores, juniors, and seniors; proportions of men and women; and proportions of full-timers and part-timers. Survey #2 yields a 65% response rate, but almost all the respondents are full-time juniors and seniors, and the group is disproportionately male. Most researchers would agree that Survey #1 has yielded "better quality" or more valid responses than Survey #2, despite its lower response rate.

This is why it's important to collect demographic information on your sample, either from the data base from which you took your mailing list or from a few questions at the end of the survey.

For the second reason that this question is almost irrelevant, suppose that despite your best efforts you only get a 30% or 40% response rate. After all the time and expense you've put in, you're not going to throw out those questionnaires, are you?

What is most important is to give your response rate in your final report and describe how representative your respondents are of the group you are studying, so your readers can judge for themselves how meritorious your survey is.

Some of your subjects will undoubtedly have bad or missing addresses on file. Opinions are mixed on whether you should delete (or replace) any subjects you cannot locate from your sample and not consider them when you calculate your response rate. Use your professional judgment to decide what is most appropriate for your particular situation.

How Can You Maximize Your Response Rate?

Four factors will probably have the most effect on your response rate:

1.   *The topic of your survey.* A survey asking for simple, non-threatening facts will probably get a higher return rate than one asking for opinions on a sensitive issue.

2.   *The people you are surveying.* You'll probably get a higher response rate if your subjects are sympathetic with your school and your project and find your project interesting and relevant, than if they find the school or project uninteresting or valueless or have negative feelings toward them. People who feel strongly about a survey topic will be more likely to respond than are those who are neutral or disinterested. Better-educated people are more likely to respond, because questionnaire surveys require a respondent to read and follow instructions.

3.   *How considerate you are of your respondents.* Recognize that you have no right to expect strangers (or even acquaintances) to go to all the

trouble of filling out a form and that they are doing you a great favor when they do. If you show your appreciation by doing all you can to minimize your respondent's trouble and make his or her job as easy as possible, he or she will be much more likely to respond to your survey and give you valid information.

4.   ***How professional and important the study appears***. If you appear professional and the study appears important, you will make your respondent's contribution seem much more worthwhile.

There is not much you can do to alter the first two factors. You probably cannot change the subject you've been asked to research or the group you've been asked to survey. The only way to handle respondent concerns about a survey on a sensitive topic is to emphasize the confidentiality and professionalism of your survey and to include the name and telephone number of someone they can contact with their questions. The only way to handle unenthusiastic subjects contacted by mail is with a convincing cover letter and perhaps a material incentive.

But you can do many things about the last two factors—***being professional and considerate of your respondents***—and therefore maximize your response rate.

To find out how *considerate* you are of your respondents, ask yourself the following:

How long is your questionnaire? The shorter it is, the more considerate you are of your respondent's time.

How long does it appear to be? A cluttered page of minuscule type looks long and complicated.

How clear are the questions? Must the respondent spend time trying to figure out what you really mean?

How clear are the directions and layout? Can the respondent move easily from one question to the next?

Was the questionnaire pilot tested? If it wasn't, you can't be sure your questions and directions are clear enough.

Which questions are first? Last? The first question should be interesting to the respondent. The long, complicated, and boring questions should be at the end, where your respondent will see that the questionnaire won't take much longer to complete.

Is a postage-paid, addressed return envelope enclosed? If it isn't, you're telling your respondents you really don't care whether you hear from them or not.

When is the survey mailed? Will it arrive at a time when your respondent is busy with other matters, such as before a weekend or holiday or during finals week?

Do you offer a summary of the findings, so your respondent can see the impact of his/her efforts?

Have you enumerated all possible reasons for people in your sample not to respond to your questionnaire? Have you done all you can to overcome those obstacles?

To find out how *professional* you appear to your respondents, ask yourself the following:

Does your questionnaire ask interesting, important-sounding questions?

Is it carefully laid-out and grammatically flawless?

Does it have a title and sponsor?

Is it well-reproduced on quality paper?

Does the cover letter convince the reader that it's worth taking the time to respond?

Will a follow-up mailing be conducted?

A great deal of research has been done on other factors affecting response rate—things like item type, print size, paper color, envelope size, etc.—often with conflicting results. It is generally accepted today that the effect of these kinds of factors varies, depending on the nature of the study and its subjects (i.e., some people under some circumstances may respond better to a survey printed on white paper, while under other circumstances, or with another group, beige paper may work better). Rather than worry about these often minor factors, concentrate instead on simply being professional and considerate of respondents. If you have reason to believe that one or more of these factors may affect your response rate significantly, test your theory in a pilot test.

What is a Questionnaire "Package"?

If you are mailing your questionnaire, you will need to prepare three additional items: a cover letter, an envelope in which to return the questionnaire, and the envelope in which you will mail everything. Each item, when properly prepared, can help motivate the respondent to answer; indeed, that's the whole purpose of the cover letter.

What Should Go into a Cover Letter?

The cover letter speaks in your absence. It says all the things you would say in person to establish and maintain a rapport with the respondent and convince the respondent to decide to complete your questionnaire. It must do all this quickly and succinctly.

There are several ways you can persuade the respondent to answer:

Make the study look important. Give people a good reason for participating. Explain the purpose of the study and why you are asking the questions you have chosen. Show that the study addresses important, interesting questions and issues (important to the respondent, not necessarily you!), and explain how the results will be used to benefit someone. If the results will not benefit the respondent directly, will they benefit his or her children? grandchildren? community? the nation?

Try to answer the question, "Why is it so important that *I* respond right *now*?" Try to give the respondent the feeling that he or she will make a real impact on something important. Stress that the respondent is part of a carefully selected sample and you *need* his or her response.

To further impress the respondent with the importance of the study, encourage an immediate response. Date the letter and set a deadline (two weeks is usually adequate).

Make the study look professional. Make the respondent feel he or she is collaborating with professional, scientific researchers who are authorities on this issue. Have the letter immaculately typed on quality letterhead paper—it conveys an official sanction of the project.

Think carefully about who should sign the letter. I hope I don't offend you by saying this . . . but it's probably not you! Nor should it be "The Technology Task Force;" most respondents won't know who this is nor care. The person signing your letter should be someone whom your respondents view as important and about whom they care. For many surveys conducted by colleges and universities, the president may be the most recognizable, influential name for most respondents. But think creatively. For some alumni surveys, for example, a highly-regarded retired faculty member may be perfect. For students, perhaps a popular professor or student life administrator may be best. For a faculty survey, perhaps the letter should be cosigned by the college president and the faculty union president (if the faculty is unionized). If your institution is lucky enough to have a famous alumna, perhaps that person would be appropriate.

Are you worried that your survey is not important enough for such important people to sign? Then ask yourself why you are doing the survey. If it's not important enough for your institution's president or a distinguished alumna to sign, is it important enough to do at all? Giving careful consideration to who signs your cover letters is a good way to make sure your surveys are carefully thought out and done only when absolutely necessary.

Regardless of who signs the letter, make sure the letter's content makes use of his or her role, background, and relation to the reader. If a retired faculty member signs a letter to alumni, for example, you might want to begin with a brief reminiscence about the "good old days," then lead into how you want to make sure today's students have just as great an experience.

Engage the respondent. Try to come up with a lead sentence that arouses interest, draws the reader in, puts the respondent in a good mood, and is vivid, emotional, interesting, and concrete. (If you can do *all* this, quit your job and start making your living writing fund-raising letters!) Some examples: "You and I share a special interest." "I need your help with a special project." "Mary Jones thought she'd never be able to go to college." Here are some other suggestions:

- Emphasize the word "you" rather than "I."

- Avoid a sleepy tone. The cover letter should be as interesting as your study and your institution.

- Consider personalizing the letter. If at all possible, have the signature handwritten, and add a handwritten "thank you!" across the bottom. A "P.S." makes the letter seem more "human."

- Consider using more than one cover letter.

Appeal to the respondent's self-interest. Try to answer the respondent's unspoken question, "What's in it for me?" If at all possible, try to get a sense of your respondents' loyalties and priorities. Then tell them what your survey is designed to discover and how that information will either benefit them directly or benefit some cause or issue they are concerned about. With adult groups, for example, you might be able to stress how your study will lead to saving taxpayers' money.

Here are some other ways to appeal to respondents' self-interest:

- Offer to send a copy of the results.

- Give a clear idea of the (short) time required to complete the questionnaire.

- Point out the (pre-addressed, postage-paid) return envelope.

Many survey researchers are finding that providing a material incentive can be an effective way to increase response rates. Material incentives may increase your response rate by giving the respondent a sense of obligation. Your incentive should be carefully chosen to have a relationship to your institution's mission and to appeal to the particular group you are surveying. (Someone I know had special "school spirit" buttons made—at some expense—and enclosed with a survey sent to graduating seniors. To his dismay, he still got a poor response rate. Obviously the buttons didn't appeal to the students.) Talk with some people in the group you will survey about an incentive that would appeal to them. Here are some possibilities:

- Enclose a pencil, a quarter, a magazine, or some other small item of value.

- Get a private donor to promise to make a charitable contribution (perhaps to a scholarship fund) if the questionnaire is returned.

- Offer free tickets to a college event if the questionnaire is returned.

- Put all returned questionnaires into a drawing for something of value (a $100 scholarship, a gift certificate from the college bookstore, a personal computer).

The effectiveness of material incentives varies; they may not always be worth the cost. To get the most value for your investment, consider using material incentives only in later mailings, with a subgroup of particular interest, when your survey makes unusual demands or intrusions, or when your survey has sensitive questions. Material incentives may be more effective if they are mentioned in the cover letter *before* you request help with your survey.

You can also appeal to the respondent's self-interest by clarifying how easy his or her role is. Give the respondent a clear idea of how long it will take to complete the questionnaire (assuming it won't take more than a few minutes). Point out that a stamped, self-addressed envelope is enclosed.

In case all else fails. . . "threaten" the respondent (mildly and in a nice way please!). Tell him or her to expect a barrage of letters, phone calls, and what-have-you if the questionnaire is not returned!

Address the issue of confidentiality. Regardless of whether your survey is anonymous, guarantee confidentiality. If your survey is totally anonymous, make this clear. If it is not, explain why. If you are using code numbers, explain their purpose. Stress that you are interested only in aggregate responses and that the respondent's questionnaire will be separated from any personal identification.

Personalize the letter. We all hate impersonal form letters. You should therefore try to personalize the letter in some way unless the topic of your survey is so sensitive that respondents will want to feel as anonymous as possible.

The best way to personalize a letter is to make it look individually-typed. This may be feasible if you have access to word processing software capable of handling a large volume of correspondence (if your office doesn't, check with your admissions office).

If you must print your cover letter, you can add touches to it to make it less cold:

- Include the name and telephone number of someone to contact should your respondents have questions about the study.

- A signature in contrasting ink, preferably hand-signed with a ball-point pen so it *looks* hand-signed.

- An offer to send a copy of the results.

Appendix 5 gives examples of cover letters that incorporate many of these suggestions.

Do You Need a Return Envelope?

Absolutely! Remember the cardinal rule: Be professional and be considerate of your respondent. Asking a respondent to provide his or her own envelope or to fold a questionnaire in a certain fashion and find a stapler or piece of tape does neither of these—and accordingly generates a lower response rate.

The return envelope should be addressed and postage-paid. To do any less tells your respondent you're not even willing to invest 32 cents to get his or her response . . . so you really don't care whether you get it or not. The envelope should be legal-sized (approximately 9 by 4 inches) so the questionnaire doesn't have to be folded an extra time to make it fit. Use a #9 envelope which will fit without folding into the #10 envelope used to mail out the questionnaire package. Some researchers have had a better response rate with a stamped envelope than a metered or business reply envelope; if you think this might affect your response rate, check it out during your pilot test.

An alternative to enclosing a return envelope is to require the student to hand-deliver his or her response as a prerequisite to receiving something of value. The most common use of this technique is with surveys of graduating seniors; students are required to hand in a completed survey before receiving their cap and gown for the commencement ceremony. The disadvantage of this approach is similar to a disadvantage of in-person administrations (covered later in this chapter): respondents may feel forced to do something they would rather not do. Some may falsify their answers as a way of rebelling against the process; others may rush through the survey at the last minute. This could adversely affect the validity of your results.

How Should the Questionnaire Package Be Assembled?

The envelope in which your questionnaire, cover letter, and return envelope are delivered conveys that important first impression. It should have a cleanly typed address or neatly aligned mailing label and an official-looking return address.

When you stuff the envelopes, discreetly number the questionnaire on a back corner and enter the same number next to the respondent's name on your master mailing list (unless you are conducting a totally anonymous survey). Fold the cover letter and questionnaire accordion-style and slip them in the envelope with the return envelope so that when the respondent opens the envelope, the first thing he or she sees is the top of the cover letter.

Why Does the Questionnaire Need a Pilot Test?

You probably think that, with all the work you've put in up to now, you've *got* to have a great questionnaire package, but you couldn't be more wrong! There's bound to be at least one question that's perfectly clear to you but confusing or misleading to respondents. Pilot-testing can be expensive and time-consuming, but it is the most important step in a survey. It is also the step most often omitted by inexperienced researchers.

Very subtle differences in question wording or format can yield dramatically different responses. Changing a question from a multiple-choice to a Likert scale, changing just a word or two, listing the questions in a different order. . .all these seemingly slight changes can have dramatic affects on responses. Pilot tests are the only way to determine which wording and format yield the most valid responses.

Pilot tests are also the best way to find out what approaches yield the highest response rate with your particular survey and group. You can test the relative effectiveness of a stamped versus a business reply envelope, a regular #10 envelope versus a large brown one, different signatories, different paper and print colors, or different cover letter approaches.

Pilot tests can be very extensive or very simple. In a full-blown pilot study, the entire survey is conducted just like the "real" one, including designing the sample and collecting, processing, and analyzing the data. The only difference is that you survey fewer people than you will in the "real" survey. This approach lets you check not only the questionnaire package but the entire research process. Full pilot studies are most often done when a project is very expensive or important.

The simplest pilot test is to hand out the questionnaire to a few people similar to those in your sample (for example, a few students if you are surveying the student body). These pilot studies are usually done with simpler, less-than-crucial studies. Ask these people not only to complete the questionnaire but also to tell you about any questions or directions they found unclear or ambiguous and how long it took them to complete the questionnaire. This gives you some feedback on your questionnaire but not on the effectiveness of the entire package. You can use this method to try out prospective questions. You can also add follow-up questions that are not planned for the final survey, to understand how respondents are interpreting the initial questions.

Once your pilot test—simple, complex, or in-between—is completed, go over the responses, looking for unexpected or inconsistent answers. If necessary, talk to some of respondents to find out why their answers were different from what you were expecting. Then revise your survey accordingly. If your pilot test leads to dramatic changes in your survey, you might want to run a second pilot test before doing the "real thing."

What is an Advance Mailing and is It Worthwhile?

Survey experts are increasingly recommending mailing an advance postcard or letter four to seven days before the questionnaire. It lets respondents know the mailing they will be getting is an important survey and not "junk mail" to be tossed out unopened. Evidence of the success of such mailings in increasing response rates is mixed, so a key question is whether the response rate increases enough to compensate for the added expense of an extra mailing. If this is a concern to you, use your pilot study to test the effectiveness of an advance mailer.

When Should the Questionnaire Package Be Mailed?

The questionnaire should arrive at a time when the respondent is least likely to be busy and tempted to put it off. This generally means timing your mailing so the questionnaire arrives on a Tuesday, Wednesday, or Thursday. Avoid questionnaire arrivals on Friday or Saturday, during midterms or finals, or during holiday or vacation periods. (Some schools, however, have had good success surveying recent graduates during the December holidays, especially if their graduates are likely to go on to further study. This is because the parents' address may be all the school has on file and the graduates are likely to be "home" then.)

What Should Be Done as the Completed Questionnaires Come Back?

Each day, count how many questionnaires are returned. Compare the code numbers you put on the back of each questionnaire against your master mailing list and check them off so these people won't receive a second mailing.

You may want to mark each questionnaire with the date of receipt. This lets you look for differences in responses between early respondents and late respondents if that is of interest to you.

Are Follow-Up Mailings Worth the Time and Expense?

Definitely! *Follow-up mailings are more effective than any other single technique in increasing response rate.* A rule of thumb is that each follow-up contact will yield an additional 50% beyond the previous contact. Thus, if you get a 40% response to your first mailing, you can expect an additional 20% from your second mailing and another 10% if you do a third—a total response rate of 70%. Follow-up mailings can therefore almost double your response rate.

Another important reason for doing a follow-up mailing is that late respondents sometimes differ from early ones. If this is true for your survey, conducting only one mailing will bias your results.

What Form Should Follow-ups Take?

Follow-ups can take many forms. You will need to select the appropriate format based on your budget and how high a response rate you are seeking. Here are some possibilities:

- Another complete questionnaire package: cover letter (amended to read, "We haven't heard from you yet!"), questionnaire, and return envelope.

- A reminder postcard or letter, asking respondents to return the questionnaire package mailed earlier (and thanking those who have already responded). This is cheaper than mailing a complete package but not as effective, since some people may have discarded or misplaced the original questionnaire.

- A complete questionnaire package sent by certified mail. This can be effective but expensive. Keep in mind that some respondents may be inconvenienced and irritated at having to travel to the post office to sign for a "dumb survey."

- A double tear-off postcard, asking the respondent to complete, tear off, and mail a postcard containing only the most crucial questions. This will generate a higher response rate than a long questionnaire, but preparing "custom" postcards like this can be expensive.

- A telephone call, either to remind subjects to answer the questionnaire or to ask at least some of the questions over the phone. The feasibility of this varies considerably depending on the nature of your questions, the nature of your telephone service (Do you have a WATS line? If you are surveying students, do students in your dorms have their own phones?) and the availability of staff to make calls.

These formats can be used in combination. You could, for example, follow an initial mailing with a reminder postcard, then with another complete package, and finally with a certified mailing or a phone call. The basic rule: persistence pays.

When Should Follow-Ups Be Mailed?

This depends on whom you are surveying and how long it will take for mail to reach them. If you are surveying students on campus, you can expect to start receiving questionnaires two or three days after you mail them. If you are surveying alumni throughout the country, you will need to allow a week for the questionnaires to get to them and another week for them to be returned.

Here is an example of a follow-up timetable for a survey of currently enrolled students:

Day 1 (Monday): Mail initial questionnaire package.

Days 2 and 3 (Tuesday and Wednesday): Questionnaires are received by students.

Days 4 and 5 (Thursday and Friday): Returns begin coming in.

Day 8 (Monday): Mail reminder postcards to everyone (thanking them if they've returned the questionnaire already).

Days 11 and 12 (Thursday and Friday): Prepare second mailing of complete package to non-respondents.

Day 15 (Monday): Mail second questionnaire package.

Day 24 (Wednesday): Begin telephoning non-respondents.

Can You Infer Anything about Non-Respondents?

Some research literature suggests that late responders (those who respond to the very last follow-ups) are similar to people who never do respond, and responses from late responders can be used to infer what the non-responders' answers would have been. Unfortunately, there is also research literature refuting this. To be safe, strive for the highest response rate possible, and don't try to infer anything about non-respondents from the responses you get.

Why Not Administer the Survey in Person?

When possible, administering a survey to your sample in person has the following advantages:

- It is cheaper; you save on envelopes and postage.

- It is faster; you don't have to wait for the mail to come through.

- You will get a higher response rate.

- You will be able to answer unanticipated questions and problems.

There are two problems with in-person administrations, however. The first problem is that you may want to survey a group that is not easily accessible in person: all undergraduates, alumni, or evening students, for example. Contacting your sample through classes, meetings, etc., will not give you a good random sample of your population.

A second problem is that respondents may feel forced to complete something they would rather not do, and this may affect their responses. If your survey is on a sensitive topic, your respondents may think a colleague might see their responses as they are being completed and adjust their answers accordingly. A respondent who would like to write a lengthy response to a question may feel pressured if he or she sees that everyone else has finished.

In-person administrations are nonetheless suitable for a variety of situations, particularly evaluations conducted at the end of a class workshop or other group activity.

How Should You Administer an In-Person Survey?

Here are some tips that will help an in-person administration yield good quality data:

- Leave off the cover letter. Prepare instead a statement to read to the group explaining the nature and purpose of the survey and soliciting their help.

- If you are administering the survey to two or more groups, keep your directions identical from one group to the next.

- Repeat key parts of your oral statement at the top of the questionnaire.

- Establish an atmosphere where respondents do not feel trapped, rushed, or otherwise uncomfortable. Don't force anyone to complete the survey.

- If other people are helping administer the survey, train them carefully so that everyone administers the survey in the same way. Try to anticipate questions so everyone will give roughly the same answers.

- Provide a large envelope or box for respondents to put their completed questionnaires in and seal it immediately, so confidentiality is preserved.

Why Not Conduct a Telephone Survey?

Sometimes a telephone survey may be preferable to a paper-and-pencil survey, depending on four factors:

Cost. If you have access to a telephone bank, low long distance rates, and a volunteer staff to make calls, a telephone survey may cost less than a mailed questionnaire survey.

Time. If you have the telephones and staff to make a large number of calls at one time, you will get faster responses than with a mailed survey. This may be a deciding factor if you need responses quickly.

Your questions. A telephone survey may be best if you have only a few questions, your questions and suggested responses are brief and simple, and/or you need to probe to get a clear open-ended response. If your questionnaire is lengthy and/or you have a fairly complex rating scale (with five or more potential responses), the questionnaire will be difficult to administer over the telephone and should be conducted as a paper-and-pencil survey.

Response rate. Both paper-and-pencil and telephone surveys can yield a high response rate; which method will get the best response from your survey depends on the nature of your survey and the people you are contacting. Do you have telephone numbers for your respondents? Will you be able to reach them or will they rarely be home when you call? It is hard to reach people who have unlisted telephone numbers, are rarely home in early evening, always leave their answering machines on, are burned out by telemarketers, are pressed for time, or are concerned about their privacy. On the other hand, it is difficult to persuade many people to take the time to complete a paper-and-pencil survey. If both methods are plausible in terms of cost, time, and question format and you are not sure which method will yield the best response rate, try both in a pilot test.

How Should You Conduct a Telephone Survey?

Entire books have been written on conducting an effective telephone survey; several are listed in the back of this book. If you are seriously interested in conducting a telephone survey, I encourage you to read one of them. In the meanwhile, here are a few tips that will help a telephone survey yield good quality data:

- Keep the survey to no more than ten minutes— preferably five.

- Keep your question formats simple, so directions can be easily understood over the phone. Use simple rating scales, seek one-word responses, and use relatively few question formats.

- Avoid many open-ended questions, unless you are only seeking a word or two; they take too long to record.

- Pre-test the interview by reading it to a few people without looking at them.

- Train the interviewers carefully and have them rehearse.

- Send an advance postcard advising respondents of the upcoming call.

- Because there is no cover letter, the advance postcard and interviewer's introduction must be convincing.

- Document the respondent's consent to participate.

- Document attempts to reach the respondent. If you reach an answering machine, leave a message explaining the purpose of your call and saying you'll try again later. Some researchers leave a toll-free 800 number where they may be reached.

- Try calling Sunday night or scheduling an "appointment" to call.

Appendix 6 gives sample materials for a telephone survey, including guidelines for the (volunteer) callers and a calling script/recording form. In the actual survey on which these materials are based, data input support was limited, so responses were coded onto generic "bubble sheets" for data entry.

If you conduct frequent telephone polls, you may wish to invest in computer-assisted telephone interview (CATI) systems that puts the script and response spaces directly on a computer screen, avoiding paper forms. (This also requires the additional expense of providing a computer for each interviewer.) CATI systems include ACS-Query, CASES, Interviewer by Info Zero Un Questionnaire Programming Language 4.0 (http.//www.gao.gov/qpl/qpl.htm), Ci3 by Sawtooth Software (708-866-0870 or 847-866-0876), Senecio Software (419-352-4371), and Telescript by Digisoft (202-289-0991). (The software industry is changing so quickly that this information may be outdated by the time you read this.)

Why Not Use Focus Groups?

A focus group is an inductive, naturalistic process of collecting qualitative data from a focused discussion by a homogeneous group. Focus groups may be preferable to a paper-and-pencil survey, depending on six factors:

Cost. A few informal focus groups may be less expensive than a questionnaire survey.

Participants. If you want to involve and inform stakeholders regarding your research, focus groups may be appropriate. On the other hand, if stakeholders are likely to have more confidence in rigorous, quantitative research, a questionnaire survey may be advisable.

Time. Focus groups may give you faster results than a mailed questionnaire survey.

Confidentiality. While you will, of course, keep participants' remarks absolutely confidential, you cannot guarantee that the participants themselves will do the same. If you are collecting information on a sensitive topic and/or the participants know one another, it may be more appropriate to use a questionnaire survey or individual interviews.

Validity. It is easier to demonstrate the reliability and validity of a survey of 500 randomly-selected students than a focus group of eight. It's difficult to provide convincing evidence that the findings from a focus group can be generalized to the entire student body.

Your questions. If you want the flexibility to explore the meaning of questions and answers, to experience the richness and diversity of respondents' opinions and beliefs, and to capture real-life data in a social environment, focus groups may be appropriate. Focus group research can give some insight into the thinking of your respondents. Focus group members use their own words and ideas, so you may discover a problem—or solution—you would not have found through a questionnaire survey. If you are designing a questionnaire survey with many open-ended questions, you may want to consider using a focus group instead. On the other hand, if you want very controlled results with everyone answering the same questions and yielding data that can be analyzed quantitatively, a questionnaire survey may be more appropriate.

There are three points at which focus groups are particularly appropriate. First, they are useful as an initial step in research. If you want to conduct a questionnaire survey to find out why students drop out, for example, you might begin with some focus groups to identify and test relevant factors on your campus.

Second, focus groups are useful to corroborate and interpret the findings of a questionnaire survey. If you find through a survey that a particular subgroup of students is less satisfied with your school than students in general, a focus group may help explain why. If you find through a survey that students are dissatisfied with a particular service on your campus, a focus group may shed light on what the problem is. If your survey yields a finding that stakeholders are likely to dispute, corroborating your finding with a few focus groups strengthens your credibility.

Third, focus groups can be useful as stand-alone research, particularly to design and evaluate a program, event, service, or experience. Focus groups can help design a brochure, evaluate an orientation program, or plan a cultural program, for example.

How Should You Conduct a Focus Group?

As with telephone surveys, entire books have been written on focus groups and qualitative research; several are listed in the back of this book. If you are seriously interested in using focus groups, I encourage you to read one of these books. In the meanwhile, here are a few tips that will help a focus group yield good quality data:

- Plan a focus group session as carefully as you would a questionnaire survey. Have a clear purpose for the session and know how you will use the results; don't let it turn into an unfocused "gripe session."

- Plan a budget as you plan your focus group. The most significant potential costs of a focus group can include renting a site, supplying trained moderators, providing audio or video recording, and offering incentives for participants to attend.

- Select a site in an environment where participants will be comfortable.

- Make sure your participants are a representative sample of the group whose opinions you want to assess.

- Write a letter (or plan a telephone call) explaining your research and convincing prospective participants to attend. Only rarely will the research topic alone be a sufficient inducement to come. You may need to offer a meal, or a gift certificate, reimburse them for travel expenses, and/or pay them outright.

- Select and train the moderators carefully. Focusing questions is an art that requires special skills. Moderators need to be trained to elicit responses from all participants and keep a talkative few from dominating the session. Write out the moderator's introduction and questions beforehand so the session stays "on track."

- Plan your questions carefully. They should be broad enough to elicit discussion, not just one-word answers, yet focused enough to make the replies useful. Some examples: "What did you think was the best part of this program?" "Tell me one way you would improve this program." "How has Bellefont College helped you be successful here?" "What do you think will be the biggest barrier to your finishing your degree?"

Focus group data can be analyzed like responses to open-ended survey questions. See the resources on qualitative data analysis and software in the "For More Information" section at the end of this book.

What Tasks Can Be Delegated to Someone Else?

Once the questionnaire and cover letter have been finalized, many of the tasks in this chapter can be delegated to support staff or a student, including any of the following:

- Arrange for duplication of questionnaires, cover letters, and envelopes.

- Arrange for mailing labels for the outer envelopes.

- Prepare the first mailing, including numbering the master mailing list and questionnaires with code numbers.

- Check off respondents as returns come in.

- Prepare subsequent mailings.

Support staff and students may also be trained to administer in-person surveys. They may also be able to edit and code responses and input data into a computer. (These tasks are discussed in the next chapter.)

Many surveys make ideal independent study projects or internships for students in business, mathematics, education, psychology, sociology, etc. Under your supervision, these students can do the entire survey from beginning to end, including:

1.   (Most important) Developing a time line to make sure the entire study can be completed in one semester or academic year.

2.   Designing and testing the questionnaire and cover letter.

3.   Selecting the random sample and arranging for mailing labels.

4.   Preparing each mailing and checking off returned questionnaires.

5.   Editing and coding the returned questionnaires and writing the code book. (This is covered in the next chapter.)

6.   Writing a computer program to analyze the data. (This is also covered in the next chapter).

7.   Writing the final report. (This is covered in Chapter 7.)

What Can a Personal Computer Do?

A personal computer is almost indispensable in completing the tasks described in this and earlier chapters:

•   As noted in Chapter 3, your questionnaire and cover letter drafts can be developed with word processing, desktop publishing, or custom survey software.

•   Your mailing list can be stored and maintained using word processing or data base software. Personal computers can also be used to assign ID numbers and can keep track of who has returned questionnaires.

•   As noted earlier in this chapter, word processing software can generate individually typed cover letters which may enhance your response rate.

•   The major statistical software packages (e.g. SAS, SPSS, Systat) are available in PC versions. If you have one of these and enough memory, you may be able to do your data analyses on your personal computer.

Chapter 5

Processing the Survey Results

Once completed questionnaires start arriving, you can begin to process the data to prepare it for statistical analysis. There are three basic steps to processing survey data: editing the responses, coding them, and getting the data entered into a computer. You will then be ready to write a computer program to *analyze* the data, a task discussed in the next chapter.

What Should You Look for as You Edit Responses?

Some respondents will not have followed directions properly; others will have marked their answers unclearly or ambiguously. The first step in processing data is therefore to review every questionnaire for inappropriate responses. Use a distinctively colored pen to mark your corrections.

Inconsistent responses. You may have a section that only Business majors were to answer, yet some other majors completed it. Cross out their responses to this section.

Multiple responses. Even though you may clearly ask respondents to check the "ONE best response," some respondents may check two or more answers to a question. There are several ways to handle this:

- Code all responses. This is usually not preferable because multiple response data are difficult to handle. Also, in doing this you are giving unfair weight to respondents who followed directions incorrectly. Had you given everyone this opportunity, other respondents may have checked more than one response too and changed your overall results.

- Delete all of the respondent's answers to the question. This is also often not preferable because you will lose data. From an empirical point of view, however, it is the most valid way to handle this situation, because you have no way of knowing which one response the respondent would have selected had he or she followed directions correctly.

91

- Choose one response at random and cross out the others. This is often preferable because you will salvage at least some information. Just make sure you choose the response *randomly*; don't always choose the first response checked.

Responses outside given categories. Suppose you have some items with possible responses of "Excellent," "Good," "Fair," and "Poor," and someone checks midway between "Excellent" and "Good." Your choices here are either to delete the response altogether or to recode the response *randomly* to either "Excellent" or "Good."

"Other" responses that really aren't. Some respondents will check an "Other—please specify" response when in fact one of the given responses suits them. Read all the "Other—please specify" comments and recode as necessary.

What is Coding?

Coding means changing every response into a number, set of numbers, or some other character or symbol. A response of "always" may be coded as "1," for example, "sometimes" may be coded as "2," and "never" as "3." Codes make it much easier for a computer to analyze data.

How Should Responses Be Coded?

Coding methods depend on the type of response requested.

Questions in which the respondent chooses the ONE best answer. Generally assign each possible answer a number and code accordingly, as in the following example:

	Code
Question 7. What is your class level?	
____ Freshman	1
____ Sophomore	2
____ Junior	3
____ Senior	4

In this example, a respondent checking "Junior" would be coded "3."

Questions in which the respondent checks all the answers that apply. For coding purposes, these questions must be treated as a series of yes/no questions, as shown here:

Code

Question 8.
What influenced you to apply to Aloysius College? Check all that apply.

___ High school guidance counselor	Question 8A.	Code "1" if checked.
___ "College night"	Question 8B.	Code "1" if checked.
___ Visit to campus	Question 8C.	Code "1" if checked.
___ Admissions brochure	Question 8D.	Code "1" if checked.

Each response is coded as if it were a separate question. Checked responses are usually coded "1"; other responses are either coded "0" or left blank. (One problem with this question format is that we can't tell if a blank means "no" or merely a skipped question.)

Open-ended questions. Coding answers to these questions (e.g., "What one thing do you like best about Northern University?") is a more subjective task than coding the questions discussed above. Here is a suggested guide:

1. Quickly read through the responses and make a list of the categories into which they fall.

2. Read through them a second time, making sure each response can be assigned to one and only one category.

3. Go through the responses a third time, this time coding them.

4. Ask someone else to go through your coding and see if he or she agrees with it.

To keep coding consistent, the entire set of responses to any one question should be coded by *one* person. The coding should then be reviewed by a *second* person to help prevent bias.

A number of software packages are available to help with this kind of qualitative data analysis, including AnSWR by the Center for Disease Control; Ethnograph by Qualis Research Associates (413-256-8835) or Qualitative Research Management

(619-329-7026); and NUD*IST by Qualitative Solutions & Research in Victoria, Australia (telephone +61(0) 3 94591699; e-mail nudist@qsr.latrobe.edu.au). See the "For More Information" section at the back of this book for a list of references on qualitative data analysis and software. With most, you enter the full responses to open-ended questions and specify certain key words that represent categories of responses. The software then scans the responses and tells you how often each key word was chosen. If your question asks, "What's the one biggest problem at this college?", your key words might include "registration," "food," and "advisement." Note that the software does not identify key words; you must still do this yourself.

What General Coding Principles Should Be Followed?

Data entry has become both simpler and more complex over the last decade: simpler, because you can now enter your data via computer screen rather than keypunch cards, yet more complex, because the many software packages for data entry all operate a bit differently from each other. It's important, therefore, to review the manual for your data entry software, or discuss the software with some knowledgeable person on your campus.

Also learn all you can about the ins and outs of uploading and downloading your data between your PC and your campus's mainframe. There are principles for data coding and entry that would be ideal for one package and system yet disastrous with another.

Given this caveat, here are some general guidelines:

1. Use numbers rather than letters or symbols (for example, code "female" as "1" rather than "F"). Some statistical programs cannot easily incorporate non-numeric codes into quantitative analyses.

2. Don't leave blanks blank. Some software packages "drop" or strip blanks, leaving you with improperly formatted, variable-length records.

3. Create separate codes for blanks and zeroes, so that non-responses are distinguished from legitimate responses of "zero." ("Zero" could be a legitimate answer to "How often did you visit the counseling center last semester?", for example.) I like to code non-responses "-1." When I'm

preparing my statistical analysis, it's easy to tell the computer to treat all -1s as missing, and they really stand out from other responses, so I can quickly tell if they've been inadvertently included.

4. Try to use numeric codes in a logical order. Coding "always" as 3, "sometimes" as 2, and "never" as 1 puts the answers into a logical continuum. (Remember that people instinctively associate larger numbers with more positive ratings.)

5. Use identical codes for questions with the same set of responses. For example, if you code one question using 4 for "strongly agree," 3 for "agree," 2 for "disagree, and 1 for "strongly disagree," use this coding scheme for all such questions.

6. Don't code decimal points, dollar signs, commas, etc. This wastes coding time and computer space. The statistical software can reinsert these symbols later.

7. Don't collapse categories to simplify your data analysis. The computer can do this for you later.

How Are the Coded Data Entered into the Computer?

Entering data into a computer is far simpler today than just a few years ago, when data had to be copied onto coding sheets and entered via keypunch cards by data entry professionals. Today, there are a number of software programs that let the novice design a set of data entry screens and delegate data entry to support staff or students. These include BLAISE, CASES, Ci3 by Sawtooth Software (847-866-0876), dBase by Borland, Epi Info, Foxpro, Paradox by Borland, P-Stat, Qbank by Teaching Technologies (800-695-0693), Query, SAS/FSP, Teleform by Cardiff Software, and SPSS's data entry program.

Software for storing and analyzing classroom test questions may also be useful; these include ExamWriter by Teacher Bytes Software (403-458-0303), LXR-Test by Logic eXtension Resources (909-980-0046), MakeTest by Mountain Lake Software (800-669-6574), MicroTest III by Chariot Software Group (800-242-7468), and Qbank by Teaching Technologies (800-695-0693). Check if any of these are available on your campus (the software market changes so quickly that some of these may be published by someone else or no longer be available by the time you read this.)

Also, many of the software packages for designing questionnaires mentioned in Chapter 3 include modules for data entry and analysis. England's Association for Survey Computing publishes a register of software for all phases of survey work; for more information, contact the ASC Secretary, P.O. Box 60, Chesham, Bucks HP5 3QH, England, telephone 01494 793033, e-mail asc@essex.ac.uk.

Keep the following in mind as you design your data entry screen:

- Use the first space to enter the respondent's ID number. When sequencing ID numbers, start with 101 or 1001 rather than 1.

- Use the next spaces to code data you have collected about the respondents other than their questionnaire responses (e.g., sex, major, geographic origin, grade point average).

- Use the remaining spaces for questionnaire responses. Checklist or multiple response items need one space for each possible answer.

You will want whoever enters your data to work quickly and accurately. They must therefore be able to read your codes explicitly, even if they are unfamiliar with your work. You can communicate your coded data in one of two ways: by transferring the data onto coding sheets from which the data entry clerks will type, or by putting data entry instructions directly on the questionnaires. We will discuss both options.

What Are Coding Sheets and How Are They Prepared?

A coding sheet (usually available in pads from your computer center) looks like a big piece of graph paper, usually 80 boxes across and 25 or so down. Data are written onto a coding sheet, one character per box, in exactly the format in which you want it entered into the computer (for example, Question 7 may code in Column 27, Question 8 in Columns 28-29, etc.).

When you transfer your data onto coding sheets, use ink, not pencil— it's easier for the clerk to read. (If you make a mistake, just draw a heavy line through that line of coding and start over on the next line.) Print neatly (a "7" can be confused with a "Y," for example) and use capital letters for all alphabetic codes. Draw a slash through the letter O (Ø) to distinguish it from a zero and make sure the letter I is distinctly different from the number 1. Some people also draw a line through the letter Z (Ƶ) to distinguish it from a 2.

How Can Data Entry Instructions Be Put Directly on a Questionnaire?

Many questionnaires can be printed with code numbers so that, after editing and perhaps coding a few open-ended items, the questionnaires can be used directly for data entry. Sometimes "bubble" sheets can be used. The advantage of these approaches is that they save you and your staff considerable coding time. But, as discussed in Chapter 3, some respondents may think that their questionnaires will go directly to a computer and that no one really cares about their individual responses, particularly written-in ones. Others may find the codes or bubble format make the questionnaire confusing. For these reasons, I prefer to use data entry codes or bubble sheets only in the limited circumstances described in Chapter 3.

There are other disadvantages to pre-coded questionnaires and bubble sheets. The chances for data entry error are greater. The temptation to skip editing is great, especially when using bubble sheets which can make editing difficult. And as you or your staff code data, you will undoubtedly catch problems that you missed when you edited the responses. Data entry staff, most likely unfamiliar with your study, will not know how to deal with these problems. They will therefore either misread and miscode the data or stop work until they can find you and ask you about the problem.

There is also something to be said for "getting your hands into the data," and nothing will do this like coding data yourself (or having a staff member familiar with the study do it). Coding forces you to look at every response, giving you new insight into your data and helping you interpret your results. You may observe unanticipated interrelationships among responses, for example, or notice firsthand that one item didn't quite work right and should be discarded.

Pre-coded questionnaires are nonetheless useful in some circumstances. Codes may be printed on the questionnaire as follows:

Multiple-choice questions:

What degree are you seeking? (8)

1 ___ Not seeking a degree
2 ___ Associate degree
3 ___ Bachelor's degree
4 ___ Master's degree

The data entry staff would key in a 1, 2, 3, or 4 in Space 8, depending on the response checked.

Checklists simply need the space numbers:

In what business subjects would you be interested in taking courses? (34-39)

___ Accounting
___ Economics
___ Finance
___ Law and Business
___ Management
___ Marketing

Here the data entry staff would key in a 1 in space 34 if the respondent checked Accounting, a 1 in space 38 if the respondent checked Management, etc. Unchecked spaces would be left blank.

Grids like Likert scales and semantic differentials can also include coding instructions, as in this item:

How would you rate...	Very Good	Good	Fair	Poor
	4	3	2	1
Advisement?	____	____	____	____(17)
The library?	____	____	____	____(18)
The quality of the labs?	____	____	____	____(19)
Faculty teaching ability?	____	____	____	____(20)

Here the data entry clerk would key in a 1, 2, 3, or 4 in each of Spaces 17-20 depending on the response checked.

If you decide to use a pre-coded questionnaire, first prepare a coding layout, just as if you were going to use coding sheets. Then mark the codes on your draft questionnaire and ask a data processing expert to review it for feasibility and clarity. Be sure to provide space and instructions for entering ID numbers and other information you have collected about the respondents outside the questionnaire.

A good data entry professional may be able to help you design a questionnaire from which data can be entered *without* pre-printed coding instructions. Discuss this possibility with your computer center.

What is a Code Book?

A code book is a few pages on which the coding scheme and data entry screens are documented. It is used to communicate this important information to your staff, your editors and coders, the data entry clerks, and your programmers to minimize confusion and misunderstandings. The code book is also invaluable if you decide to repeat your study or do a follow-up on it.

A code book lists the name of every piece of information you are putting on the computer, in which space it is located, its format (numeric, alphabetical, etc.) and the meaning of each code. Here is an example:

Data element	Space	Format	Codes/Other information
ID number	1	999	
Sex	2	A	M = male
			F = female
Grade point avg	3	9V99	
Question 1	4	9	1 = Always
			2= Sometimes
			3 = Never
Question 2	5	99	Amount spent on food

The Format column uses "computerese" notation: "9"s are used to show the data are numeric; a "V" is inserted wherever a decimal point should go. This tells the computer programmer, for example, that a grade-point average stored in the computer in Space 3 as "326" should be read and printed as "3.26."

Chapter 6

Analyzing the Survey Data

Statistical software such as SPSS and SAS have brought a myriad of statistical analysis techniques to the fingertips of even the novice researcher. While this capability gives the researcher a great deal of power, it also means he or she can be overwhelmed with the plethora of statistical analyses available. This chapter is designed to help you make your choices. It has been written for those with at least a modest familiarity with statistical techniques. If you are a novice with statistics, I suggest you find a statistical consultant (perhaps a faculty member) to help you analyze and interpret your data.

Before you choose your analyses, you need to know what kind of data you have: categorical, ordered, or scaled (See Chapter 1 for an explanation of those terms). You also need to know what information you would like from your data. In particular, you need to decide if you simply want to *describe* your group or if you want to try to *explain* why your group responded or behaved in a particular way. Describing is a simpler task than explaining, so we'll discuss that first.

Do You Simply Want to *Describe* Your Group?

If you want to describe your group with a *chart or graph* of responses, use the chart below to choose the appropriate method.

What do you want to do?	What kind of data do you have?	Use this method
Examine the responses of one group to one question	Scaled or ordered	Frequency distribution, bar graph, line graph
	Categorical	Frequency distribution, bar graph
Compare the responses to two groups to one question	Any kind	Paired frequency distribution or graphs
Compare the responses of one group to two questions	Ordered or categorical	Cross tabulation table
	Scaled	Scattergram

If you want to describe your group with *statistics*, use the chart below to choose the appropriate statistics.

What do you want to describe?	What kind of data do you have?	Use this statistic
The average response to a question	Scaled	Mean or median
	Ordered	Median
	Categorical	Mode
The spread or variability of responses to a single question	Scaled	Standard deviation
	Ordered	Semi-inter-quartile range or range
	Categorical	Proportion falling outside mode
The degree of the relationship between responses to two questions	Scaled	Pearson's product-moment correlation coefficient
	Ordered	Spearman rank-order correlation coefficient
		Spearman rank-order correlation Kendall tau coefficient
	Categorical	Cramer's index of contingency
The degree of relationship among responses to three or more questions	Scaled	Multiple correlation Partial correlation
	Ordered	Kendall partial rank correlation

How Well Do Your Sample Results Correspond to the Views of the Entire Student Body?

When researchers analyze survey data, we want to be able to assume that our sample results are similar to those we would get if we were able to survey every student. Suppose, for example, that we surveyed 400 students and found that 58% of them are "satisfied" with the current registration process. We would like to be able to say that 58% of *all* students at our college are satisfied with the registration process.

Assuming we surveyed a random sample of students, can we say this? No! It's very unlikely that *exactly* 58% of the entire student body is satisfied with the registration process. It's possible that the overall percentage is really 59%, 58%, maybe even 63%. This discrepancy between our 58% and the true percentage is called *sample error* (first discussed in Chapter 1). It is not really an "error," just a phenomenon that exists because even a good random sample is unlikely to match *precisely* the entire group.

When reporting your results, you will be much more professional and credible if you mention the possible sample error of your findings. For example, instead of simply saying "58% of students are satisfied with the registration process," say, "58% of students are satisfied with the registration process *with an error margin of plus or minus 6%.*" Statisticians know this means that you are 95% sure that between 52% and 64% of students are satisfied with the registration process.

How is the Error Margin Calculated?

When are you reporting *percentages*, this formula will give you a good estimate of the error margin:

$$\sqrt{\frac{1}{n}} \times 100\% \quad \text{where } n = \text{your sample size}$$

In the example above, we surveyed 400 students, so the error margin was

$$\sqrt{\frac{1}{400}} \times 100\% = \sqrt{.0025} \times 100\% = .05 \times 100\% = 5\%.$$

While you can use this formula to find the error margin of any percentages you have, it will slightly overestimate the error margin of percentages close to 0% or 100%. If you want a more accurate error margin in these cases, look in any statistics textbook for a discussion of "confidence intervals for proportions."

Error margins can also be calculated for means, for differences between two means, and for differences between two proportions. To find out how, again look in any statistics textbook for "confidence intervals."

Do You Want to Try to *Explain* Why Your Group Responds or Behaves in a Certain Way?

This is a more interesting kind of analysis than simply describing your results. Statistical analyses are available to help you answer the following kinds of questions:

- Is my group different from an established or theorized norm?

- Is my sample truly representative of my population?

- Are two or more subgroups different from each other?

- Are two or more responses from my group different?

- Has my group changed over a period of time?

- Are there any interrelationships among my group's responses?

The statistical analyses that answer these questions are *hypotheses tests*. Hypothesis tests follow six steps:

1.   An hypothesis is made about the results. To keep things simple, the hypothesis is usually that there is *no* difference, relationship, etc., even if you're actually hoping or expecting that there *will* be a difference.

2.   The hypothesis is initially assumed to be correct.

3.   A statistical analysis is done to find out the probability of getting our sample results if the hypothesis is true.

4.   If there is a reasonable probability that we'd get our sample results, we conclude the hypothesis may be true and that there is no evidence of a difference, relationship, etc.

5.   If it's very unlikely (usually less than a 5% or 1% chance) that we'd get our sample results, either our sample results are wrong or the hypothesis is wrong. Since our sample data are from a well-planned, valid study (this

is why it's important to have a valid study!), we conclude that the *hypothesis* is what's wrong and that there is a *statistically significant* difference, relationship, etc.

6.   The astute researcher knows that *statistical* significance may be insufficient for *practical* significance. If you are surveying thousands of people, a statistically significant difference may be so small that it has no real-world, practical significance. Only your good professional judgement can tell you if a statistically significant difference has practical significance.

The rest of this chapter is a guide to choosing the statistical analyses most appropriate for your data and the questions you have about them. As I've mentioned before, if you are a statistical novice, you may want to ask a statistical consultant to help you choose your analyses and interpret them.

Do You Want to See if Your Group is Different from an Established Norm or a Theorized Value? Or Do You Want to See if Your Sample is Truly Representative of Your Population?

You will probably want to see, for example, if respondents to a faculty survey differ from all the faculty at your school in terms of such factors as sex, rank, tenure status, department or division, and highest degree. Or you might want to see if students at your school differ from national norms.

If your data are *scaled*, use a t-test for one mean.

If your data are *ordered*, use a Kolmogorov-Smirnov one-variable test.

If your data are *categorical*, use a chi-square test for goodness of fit or a t-test for one proportion.

Do You Want to See if Two or More Subgroups are Different from Each Other?

You might want to see, for example, if there's a difference between men and women or among freshmen, sophomores, juniors, and seniors. Use the following chart to choose the appropriate analysis.

What kind of data do you have?	How many subgroups do you have?	Use this analysis
Scaled	Two	t-test for two independent means
	Three or more	one-way analysis of variance
Ordered	Two	Mann-Whitney U test
	Three or more	Kruskal-Wallis one-way analysis of variance
Categorical	Two	t-test for two proportions
	Two or more	chi-square test of association

Do You Want to See if Two or More Responses from Your Group are Different? Or Do You Want to See if Your Group Has Changed Over a Period of Time?

You might want to compare for example, your students' ratings of the math department and the computer science department to see if they differ. Or if you have been following a group of alumni over a period of time, you might want to compare their perceptions five years ago to their perceptions today. Use the following chart to choose the appropriate test.

What kind of data do you have?	How many responses do you want to compare?	Use this analysis
Scaled	Two	t-test for matched pairs
	Three or more	one-way analysis of variance
Ordered	Two	sign test
		Wilcox on matched pairs signed ranks test
	Two	Friedman two-way analysis of variance
Categorical	Two	McNemar test for significance of changes
	Three or more	Cochran Q test

Do You Want to Look for Interrelationships Among Your Group's Responses?

The analysis you choose will depend on the kind of data you have and the kind of relationship you wish to examine. Sometimes researchers are interested in the general interrelationship among two or more responses. More often, however, they are particularly interested in the relationship of one or more responses to *one particular* response or factor. A researcher might want to study, for example, the relationship of several questionnaire responses to grade-point average. Or the researcher might want to study the relationship of several questionnaire responses whether or not a student drops out, whether or not a student flunks out, or responses to one question asking for overall satisfaction with Western College. Both kinds of analyses are discussed in the sections that follow.

Do You Want to Study the Relationship of Several Responses to One Particular Response or Factor?

You can use multivariate analysis of variance, regression analysis, or discriminant analysis to do this.

If you want to study the relation of responses to two or more *categorical* questions to responses to one *scaled* question, use multivariate analysis of variance. This analysis would be used, for example, if you wanted to study the relation of sex, age group, and major to grade-point average.

If you want to study the relation of one or more *scaled* responses to another *scaled* response, use regression analysis. This analysis could be used, for example, if you wanted to study the relation of several scaled responses to responses to one question asking for overall satisfaction with college.

If you want to study the relation of two or more *scaled* responses to one *categorical* (usually dichotomous) response, use discriminant analysis. This analysis would be used, for example, if you used several scaled responses to distinguish between students who drop out and students who return.

If all the data you're studying are scaled, you have a real choice between analysis of variance and regression analysis. Consider these points as you make your decision:

Analysis of variance is actually a broad term covering many different kinds of analyses. You can look for differences among several responses made by one group, differences in responses among several subgroups, or simultaneously examine differences within and among subgroups. You can also use Scheffe contrasts to see *how* the responses affect the response in which you're most interested. For more information on these kinds of analyses, consult a textbook on experimental design.

Regression analysis is usually used with just one group but gives you a lot more information. In particular, it lets you *predict* the response of most interest to you from the other responses you're studying. You might predict grade-point average, for example, from responses to several scaled questions. Regression analysis will also let you measure the accuracy of your predictions and give you information on the relative importance of several responses to the item of most interest to you.

Do You Simply Want to Examine the Relationship Among Responses to Two or More Questions?

You can use correlation tests, chi-square tests, or factor analysis to do this.

If you want to see if there is a relationship between *two scaled* responses, use Fisher's z test for the Pearson correlation coefficient.

If you want to see if there is a relationship between *two ordered* responses, use a test of significance for Spearman's correlation coefficient.

If you want to see if there is a relationship between *two categorical* responses, use a chi-square test of association.

If you want to study the interrelation among a *large set of scaled* responses, use factor analysis. It "reduces" the responses into factors or components. Researchers use factor analysis to (1) explore relations among responses, (2) test hypotheses or theories about what the interrelationships should be, and (3) reduce a large number of responses to a manageable few for further study.

How Should Census Data Be Analyzed?

Virtually all the statistical analyses presented in this chapter are *inferential* statistics, designed to be used to make an inference from a sample to an entire population. What if you have conducted a census, collecting data on everyone in your group rather than just a sample? There are three schools of thought on how to handle this:

1. Since the data are from a census, they are completely accurate. Any difference, however small, is a real difference and therefore significant. No inferential statistics—hypothesis tests or error margins—are required.

2. Although the data are from a census and all differences are therefore *statistically* significant, some differences may not be large enough for *practical* significance. Hypothesis tests and error margins help eliminate the very small differences with no practical significance.

3. Although the data are from a census at one point in time, they are being used to make inferences about future populations which will be slightly different. A census of the Fall 1997 student body, for example, might be used to make decisions affecting the Spring 1998 student body, which would be somewhat different. Under such circumstances, the Fall 1997 student body would be considered a sample of all students, present *and* future. Inferential statistics including hypothesis tests and error margins are therefore appropriate.

How Should You Check If Your Respondents Represent the Group From Which They're Taken?

As has been already noted several times, if anyone is to have any confidence in your results, it's important that your respondents be representative of the group from which they were taken. If 45% of the group you're sampling from is female, for example, about 45% of your respondents should be female. (They don't have to be *exactly* 45% female, however; they can be a little more or a little less. Statistical analyses will tell you how far from 45% is *too* far to match.)

If you survey a sample of your student body, your respondents should match the student body in terms of their breakdown by sex, racial/ethnic status, class level, major, full-time/part-time status, and any other factor you consider important. If you survey a sample of your faculty, your respondents should match the faculty in terms of such factors as sex, highest degree, rank, tenure status, department or division. (The number of factors you examine depends on the how sensitive your survey is and how much the results will be challenged. If you are comparing subgroups, such as men and women, you should also check how representative each subgroup is.)

Documenting the representativeness of your sample is thus an important component of your statistical analysis. How can you do this?

If your data are *scaled*, use a t-test for one mean. For example, use this test to see if your respondents' overall grade-point average is significantly different from the overall grade-point average of the student body.

If your data are *ordered*, use a Kolmogorov-Smirnov one-variable test. You could use this test, for example, to see if your faculty respondents' average highest degree is significantly different from the average highest degree of the faculty as a whole.

If your data are *categorical*, use a chi-square test for goodness of fit or a t-test for one proportion. You could use a chi-square test, for example, to see if the distribution of faculty respondents across academic divisions is significantly different from the distribution of the entire faculty. You could use a t-test to see if the proportion of tenured faculty respondents is significantly different from the proportion of tenured faculty among the entire faculty.

What Else Should You Consider as You Choose Your Analyses?

Perhaps the most important thing you should keep in mind is that even statistical experts often disagree on the most appropriate analysis for a given set of data. Don't let this chapter dictate what you do. If you have doubts about the appropriate analysis for a particular situation, consult some statistics textbooks or someone knowledgeable about statistics.

Another thing to keep in mind is that the analyses listed here can be used with "higher level" data. Analyses suggested for categorical data, for example, can be used with ordered or scaled data. Analyses suggested for ordered data can be used with scaled data as well.

This often gives you a real choice among analyses. In most cases, the preferable analysis will be the parametric one designed for *scaled* data. Parametric analyses (the term was discussed in Chapter 1) usually have the following advantages:

1. Parametric analyses are the *most well-known*. Your reader is more likely to be familiar with analysis of variance than the Cochran Q test, for example. Using a familiar test will make your results easier for your reader to understand.

2. Parametric analyses usually provide *more information*. Most of them, for example, are designed to provide information that can help you understand why individuals vary from the mean. This information can be very helpful in understanding your results.

3. Parametric analyses are *more powerful*. This means that when you decide that there is no significant difference, relationship, etc., you have a better chance of being right than if you've used an analysis designed for categorical or ordered data.

4. Parametric analyses are *more robust* or flexible. While they are usually based on assumptions about the data, the assumptions can often be violated without affecting the validity of your results. Many of these analyses can be used, for example, with ordered data even though they are designed strictly for scaled data. Analysis of variance technically

assumes that each set of responses you are comparing comes from a separate group, but it is robust enough that you can use it to compare three or more responses from one group.

Don't forget, by the way, that dichotomous data can be treated as scaled data. You can often convert one categorical response into a set of dichotomous (yes/no) responses in order to use an analysis designed for scaled data. Chapter 1 discusses dichotomous data, and Chapter 5 discusses coding these "dummy variables."

A final note: Many of these analyses have limitations and restrictions to their use beyond what can be addressed here. Before you use any of these tests, read up on them in a statistics textbook to make sure the ones you choose are appropriate to use with your data.

How Should the Results of a Statistical Analysis Be Reported?

There are five elements that should be included in the write-up of any statistical analysis:

1.   The purpose of the statistical analysis;

2.   The basic, descriptive statistics you found (usually means or percents);

3.   Whether or not the statistics are statistically significantly different;

4.   The results of the statistical test (this is generally presented in parentheses giving the "test statistic" and, if the results are statistically significant, the probability); and

5.   Your conclusion.

Here are two examples:

To find out if time spent studying was related to the decision to leave Maryville College before graduating, students were asked how many hours they study in a typical week. Students still enrolled studied an average of 9.8 hours per week; students who left studied an average of 6.4 hours. These means are statistically significantly different (t(34)= 5.79, $p < .01$). There therefore appears to be a relation between how much students study and their decision to leave Maryville.

To see if respondents matched the overall student body in terms of major, their majors were compared with the majors of the entire student body. Of the respondents, 35% were science majors, 23% were education majors, 29% were business majors, and 13% were majoring in other fields. Overall, 37% of Maryville students are science majors, 27% are education majors, 25% are business majors, and 11% are majoring in other fields. The respondents' majors do not differ significantly from Maryville students' majors as a whole ($\chi^2(3) = 0.86$). The respondents therefore appear to be representative of Maryville students as a whole in terms of major.

Your report may not include paragraphs written exactly like this; you may choose, for example, to present a series of results of statistical tests together, or you may find a table more effective than text for presenting your figures. But the five elements listed above should be presented *somewhere* in your report so that your readers can understand your results. Writing an effective report is discussed in more detail in the next chapter.

What Else Should Go into the Data Analysis Computer Program?

The data analysis program should have several additional elements:

A listing of the raw data. This will help you find and correct coding and keying errors.

Edit checks. Always ask for frequency distributions of every response. This will give you a quick picture of your data and help you identify bad data or codes. You may also want to ask for two-way tables ("cross-tabs"), showing the frequency distributions of two items together, to identify inconsistent answers. For example, you might want to compare sex and participation in men's and women's sports.

Reliability and validity checks. Making reliability and validity checks of your items was discussed in Chapter 4. Include a check on the "representativeness" of your sample respondents. Plan to compare the characteristics of your respondents (e.g., proportions of men, freshmen, business majors) with known characteristics of the group from which you took your sample.

Data transformations. You will want to make the following minor changes to your data before you analyze them:

- Identify missing data. Blank or missing data should be clearly identified and then deleted from data analysis. An important exception: blanks in checklists are valid responses and should *not* be identified as missing.

- Reverse inversely coded items. If you have a Likert or semantic differential scale, probably some items are positive and others are negative. If you coded the response columns 1, 2, 3, and 4, have the computer reverse the codes of the negative items (changing 1 to 4, 2 to 3, 3 to 2, and 4 to 1). This will make it easier to compare responses.

- Create new variables. You may want to "collapse" some categories into which few people fell, add up several numbers to a total, and so on.

Data labeling and documentation. Provide plenty of labels, headings, and such so your printout will be easy to read. Put in enough notes that your data transformations will be easily understood.

What Software is Available to Analyze the Data?

A large number of statistical software packages are available to analyze data on either a large "mainframe" computer or right on your personal computer, including SPSS, SAS, BMDP, Minitab, and Systat. Inquire which are available at your computer center. Most of these can be self-taught, and there is almost certainly someone on your campus familiar with them and able to help you. "Mainframe" software is preferable if you have a large data base or if your computer center will provide data entry staff and other support. If your data base is small enough for your PC to handle, support from your computer center is limited, and you have the staff to handle data entry, you may find you will get your analysis done more quickly if you do it yourself on your own PC.

How Should the Data Be Stored?

Your data will need to be stored in such a way that you preserve the confidentiality of your respondents' answers and don't betray their trust. There are actually three sets of data to be stored securely: the master mailing list, the questionnaires themselves, and the coded data.

The master mailing list, the one that relates respondents' names to their ID numbers (and thus links names with responses), should be stored *very* securely. Don't leave it on a hard drive or in a mainframe if there is any chance of an unauthorized person accessing it.

The questionnaires should be saved because the written-in responses will be useful in interpreting data analyses, writing the final report, and answering questions from people who read the final report. If the questionnaires have identifying information on them (e.g., social security numbers), they should also be stored securely.

Computerized data may be stored on computer tape (if they are being handled by your computer center) or on a diskette (if you're doing the data entry and analysis on your personal computer). Once the data have been thoroughly checked and edited, you may want to have the ID numbers "stripped" (deleted) to guarantee the confidentiality of the data even further. If you are using a personal computer to analyze your data, put the data on a diskette and store it in a locked cabinet when you're not using it.

Chapter 7

Reporting the Survey Results

The final aspect of conducting a survey is communicating the findings clearly and accurately so they can be used for decision making. Your report should be planned as carefully as any other part of the survey research process. Otherwise, no one will use your findings and your work on this project will have been for naught.

Who Will Read and Use Your Findings?

Before you begin any writing, you should know whom you are addressing. Although, in a well-done survey, you probably sat down with members of your intended audience when you began planning the survey, it's a good idea to sit down with them again after you have the data in hand but before you write your report. Find out the following:

What is your readers' frame of reference? Do they have a broad understanding of your institution, or do they see everything only in terms of their own responsibilities? Do they understand and appreciate your institution's history, values, culture, and environment? Are they aware of the relative strengths and weaknesses of your students, your programs, and your resources?

What are their needs? What kind of support and help would they like from you? Is their most pressing need for more resources, more attention, or more respect? Do they want support for the status quo or for initiating change?

Are they already familiar with what you have been doing, or will they need a complete description of what research was done?

Do they have time to study an extensive report, or will they want only a short summary?

Will they want only your findings and recommendations, or will they want to know how you arrived at your conclusions?

Are they knowledgeable about empirical research methodology, or will you need to explain what you did in layperson's language?

Are they likely to criticize the study? Will you need to anticipate their criticisms and incorporate responses into your report?

Are they likely to be questioned about the study by others? Will they need sufficient details to respond to others' concerns?

In What Form Do Your Readers Need the Findings?

As you plan and write your report, you will have to wrestle with two seemingly contradictory needs of your readers: your report must be the essence of brevity, yet include all the details they consider important. Your primary challenge will be to reconcile these two disparate needs.

Sit down again with members of your intended audience to review what you think are your key findings and discuss how they might be best presented. Listed below are some of the forms your report may take, depending on which is more important to your readers—their need for brevity or their need for information—and how knowledgeable and interested they are in empirical research. Also find out if they prefer to absorb information through text, numbers, graphs, or oral presentations.

Whatever format(s) you decide on, it's a good idea to develop a dissemination plan, describing the information to be shared, the format, the date of distribution, and the people receiving the report. This helps ensure that all the relevant aspects of your research are shared appropriately and no one is inadvertently left off your mailing list. Dissemination plan formats include:

A few tables summarizing your findings. If your readers are already familiar with your study, it may be sufficient to make up a few tables highlighting your principal findings and pass them around. But some people have difficulty understanding tables, and your charts may not be all that clear. In such cases, a couple of brief explanatory paragraphs accompanying your tables may make a much better report.

An executive summary. This is a one- or possibly two-page summary of your study. It's a distant cousin of the abstract used in scholarly research. The major difference is that, while an abstract summarizes the entire study, the executive summary emphasize findings, especially those that will be of most interest to decision makers.

An executive summary should be the first page of any lengthy report sent to busy people. It can also be sent out alone, with an offer to provide the complete report on request. (Don't be dismayed at how few people take you up on your offer!)

The executive summary may be widely read and quoted. It's therefore important to select carefully the points to be communicated in the summary and to do so in a form that is attractive and easy to understand.

A complete report. Many survey research projects require a complete report that documents what you did, why you did it that way, and all your findings and conclusions. Some of your readers will want a complete report, if only to have on file or to skim for parts of interest to them. Even if the complete report is sent to no one, it's a good idea to prepare one and keep it in your files or in the University archives to answer any questions and to serve as a resource should anyone decide to conduct further research on the topic. If your study was funded by anyone, the sponsor should get a complete report.

A short report. A shorter version of the full report can give more detail than the executive summary without burdening readers with a full report. If your complete report runs more than ten pages and an executive summary won't get your points across, you'll probably need a short version of it to get your message across to decision makers.

Supplemental reports. These are an excellent way to get some of the nuances and details of the study to only those people who would be really interested. For example, if you are doing a survey of student satisfaction with your college, you might send only to the student life staff details of the findings on satisfaction with dorm life. You might send only to the computer center staff or computer science faculty details of the findings on satisfaction with computer access.

An oral presentation. This can be a very effective way to share your study with people who want only highlights and don't like dealing with tables of statistics or dry text. You may have difficulty, however, in convincing the powers-that-be to give you time to make your presentation. Try distributing an executive summary first and then offering to make a presentation. You'll find that, after making successful (i.e., short and interesting) presentations to just a few groups, your track record will open doors to other groups. There are bound to be some groups on campus who are anxious for information or an interesting program; offer to speak to them.

More than one report. You may need to plan different reports for different audiences. You may prepare a complete report with an executive summary for chief decision makers, a shorter report to the faculty discussing only those findings of direct interest to them, a very brief summary for the public relations office to use in press releases, and an oral presentation to a committee or task force.

What Are the Components of a Survey Research Report?

A complete report should include each of the following elements:

A meaningful title. Often the title alone must convince your audience to read your report. Your title should therefore explain what your report is about and help convince them to read it. "Student Survey Results" says nothing; "Factors Related to Student Retention" says much more. Questions ("Why Do Students Drop Out?") can pique readers' curiosity. (Make sure the readers can quickly skim the report and find the answer!) Some of the best titles condense the principal findings of the study: "The Impact of Faculty/Student Interactions in Reducing Student Attrition."

The author, originating office, and date. Someone will pull out your report from a file five or ten years from now, and your cover memo will have vanished. It's amazing how useless a report is if no one can remember who did it or when. Consider carefully who should be listed as author. While you may have done the actual work (and you should receive credit for that, at least in the body of the report or a footnote), it may be more prudent to show the report as being released by, say, a task force or a vice president's office. If these entities are more visible than you are, the report may be given more attention. If the results are controversial, it may be wise to distance yourself a bit from the report.

Acknowledgments. If anyone provided financial support for your study, helped with the mechanics, assisted with data entry and analysis, or helped in any other way, it's only courteous to acknowledge that assistance and express appreciation for it . . . especially if you'd ever like their help again!

An executive summary gives a quick overview of why and how the study was done and highlights principal findings and implications. Be careful to reflect the results accurately in this summary. The temptation to oversimplify or overreach for meaning is great and, as noted earlier, the executive summary is most likely to be widely circulated and quoted.

The purpose of the study. To orient your reader, you should explain why the study was done, what it was designed to find out, and how the results might be used. This explanation may be only a sentence or two.

Depending on the nature of your study and your audience, you may want to include some background information to help orient your reader further. If you are doing a survey related to student retention, for example, you may want to give a brief summary of the literature on factors related to student retention. If you are doing a survey related to some other campus problem, you may want to give a brief history of circumstances leading up to the study.

How the study was done. Write at least a few sentences explaining how your data were collected. The following points are crucial for the reader to decide on the validity and usefulness of your results and should be included in any report, short or long:

- The group you took your sample from (e.g., all full-time freshmen as of Fall, 1996).

- How the persons contacted were selected.

- The number of people contacted, the number responding, and the response rate.

- Any evidence that the people who responded are a representative, unbiased sample of the group you wanted to survey.

- Whether the questionnaire was distributed by mail or in person.

- The date the survey was conducted.

- Any caveats that readers should keep in mind as they interpret the findings. These might include cautions about a low response rate, a response group that is not quite representative of the overall group you wanted to survey, or anything that has happened since the survey was conducted that might affect results were it repeated today.

Most readers will be more interested in your results than your methodology, so this section should probably be rather short. Be sure to include information on how to contact you so anyone interested in more information can obtain it.

Results. This is the part of your report on which most readers will concentrate. Since it is also the most complicated, this section requires careful thought and planning so that it may be clearly understood by all your readers, regardless of their knowledge of research methods and statistical analyses.

Your readers will find your results easier to follow if they are broken into the following clearly labeled sections:

- *An overall descriptive summary of your results.* This is the part of your report on which most readers will concentrate. It therefore requires careful writing to keep it clear.

  Since "a picture is worth a thousand words," the best way to communicate your basic findings is often to include a copy of the actual questionnaire with the results filled in. If you don't include the actual questionnaire, the questions that produced the results should be quoted exactly, since small differences in wording can produce large differences in responses.

  For many items on the questionnaire, you'll want to fill in the percentage who checked response A, the percent who checked response B, and so on. Do not give the *number* of people who checked A and the number who checked B; these figures are meaningless. Convert your counts into percentages; most people are more used to dealing with them than decimals.

  With Likert scales, you have several choices on how to report results. First, you may wish to report the percentage of respondents choosing each rating (e.g., 15% rated the program "excellent," 28% rated the program "very good," etc.).   I'm not too fond of this report method, however, because there will be too many figures for many people to assimilate.

For many in your audience, it may be sufficient to report simply the percentage who responded "strongly agree" or "agree," or who chose "excellent" or "very good."   While this report format is sufficient for many audiences, I'm not too fond of it either, because it eliminates some potentially useful information (I like to see the percentage who chose "poor," for example.).

My preference is to compute the mean or median rating for each item and mark an X on the scale to show the spot where the mean or median falls. With this method, even mathophobes can quickly scan a rating scale and get a good sense of what the ratings were like.

If your questionnaire asks respondents to write in a numerical rating from a scale given at the top of the page, you can report a mean rating for each item, but some of your readers will find this difficult to follow. If your readers are largely well-versed in statistics, however, this method can be effective, and reporting standard deviations will give a sense of which items have the most consistent ratings.

You might want to include some "typical" responses to open-ended questions in this section.

While this first section of the results should be statistically simple, it should include the margin of error discussed in the previous chapter. This figure is essential for your readers to judge which differences are truly meaningful.

• *More detailed results.*   If your results are at all extensive, the overall results section will be followed with findings for subgroups, findings of interest to only a few readers, and special analyses such as correlations among responses and the results of statistical tests. (Examples of how to present the results of statistical tests are given in Chapter 6.)

These sections should be clearly labeled so that readers can skip them if they like. Headings should describe the point of the analysis ("Factors Affecting Grade Point Average") rather than the analysis itself ("Results of Multiple Regression Analysis").

Avoid the temptation to report every single statistical analysis you conducted. If it doesn't make a meaningful contribution to your conclusions, leave it out.

These are not the sections for subjective discussions or interpretations. Although people may be interested in your opinions about the results, they have the right to be able to look at the pure statistics, unsullied by anyone's beliefs, and draw their own conclusions.

- **Tables and graphs.** You will probably do a much better job of communicating your findings to your readers if you present some of the data in tables or graphs. A well-constructed table will permit the reader to quickly and easily find and compare figures of interest to him or her. Hints for creating a well-designed table or graph are given later in this chapter.

Conclusions and recommendations. In this section, draw your conclusions from your findings and your statistical analyses. Your conclusions should clearly relate your data to the questions addressed by your study and described in the introduction to the report. This section may also include the following:

- **Speculations** on possible reasons why your findings turned out the way they did. Do this only if you don't mind being wrong! Discuss your ideas with colleagues before you include them to make sure they make sense. One way to do this is by sharing a "preliminary draft--subject to change" report with a few key colleagues.

- **Recommendations for actions** that might be taken based on your findings. Institutional researchers have strong disagreements about whether it is their place to make recommendations. Recommendations do help drive home the major conclusions from your study, but they can also create problems for you. By implying that something can be improved, recommendations leave an inference that something is presently not as good as it should be, and this is very likely to offend whoever is responsible for that area. Unfettered recommendations can result in challenges about the quality of your research and a serious undermining of your credibility.

If you don't want your recommendations to get you in trouble:

o   Praise as well as criticize. Include a positive conclusion for every problem you uncover.

o   Keep your recommendations non-controversial ("More encourage-ment for student independent study projects is needed.").

o   Confirm an already accepted problem ("More parking space is urgently needed.").

o   Phrase your recommendations gently. Rather than say "The college should provide more activities on weekends," say, "Further research may be needed into the appropriateness of the college's weekend activities."

o   Don't phrase your recommendations in such a way that anyone reading them might feel threatened or defensive. Avoid pinning blame on any one department.

o   If your study unearths a problem in a particular area, talk to the person in charge of that area before your report is released. At the very least you will have forewarned the supervisor. More likely you will gain some insights that help explain your findings and possibly change your recommendation. The supervisor may tell you he or she is aware of the problem and is delighted to see support from you for resources to help address it.

o   If some of your conclusions or recommendations are *very* sensitive (if, for example, you identify evidence of sex discrimination in a particular department), omit the most sensitive details from your written report and instead discuss them in person with those who should be aware of the problem. Remember that your study only provides *indications* of a problem, not *proof* of it.

- ***Suggestions for further research.*** Any good study raises mo questions than it answers. Note if you are planning on studying the issues further. You may have some ideas for someone else who wou be interested in conducting further research. I call this section "Lookii Ahead," and it's a nice way to end the report.

How Else Can You Keep Your Report Readable, Interesting, and Useful?

Your report is not a journal article. While your readers are probably intelligent a well-educated, chances are that many are not familiar with research methodolog statistics, or the subject of your study. Even if they are, they probably don't ha time to study a scholarly missive. Here are some suggestions for ways to impro the readability of your report.

Have it tell a story with a meaningful point. Consider this paragraph from report on one college's participation in the ACE/UCLA Cooperative Institution Research Program's survey of incoming freshmen:

> Between 78% and 80% of Lawndale College freshmen relied on family financial support. Lawndale freshmen were more likely to have student loans (48%) than freshmen nationally. Only 57% were dependent on grants, compared to 92% nationally.

What's the point of this paragraph? I don't know, and if I don't, the repor readers probably don't either, and they aren't going to spend time puzzling it ou

On the other hand, consider these paragraphs from a similar survey:

> Freshmen women enter Richmond University with a stronger academic background, on average, than men. They have earned higher average high school grades and have spent more time in high school talking with their teachers, volunteering, studying, and participating in student clubs and groups. Freshmen men, on the other hand, are more likely to not have completed high school homework on time and to have come late to class. They have spent more time in high school playing sports, watching television, and working. Freshman women are more likely

attending college to "gain a general education," "learn more about things," "become more cultured," and "prepare for graduate study." Men are more likely attending to "make more money." It is more important to freshman women than men to help others in difficulty, influence social values, and promote racial understanding, while it is more important to men to "be very well off financially."

Despite women's stronger preparation for college, however, men rate themselves higher in intellectual self-confidence, mathematics ability, competitiveness, originality, popularity, social self-confidence, physical health, and emotional health. (Women rate themselves higher than men in "understanding of others.")

The message from these paragraphs is (I hope) clear: women at Richmond University have a stronger preparation for college, but men have greater self-confidence. Freshman men and women at this school will both need help adjusting to college, but of vastly different kinds. (These kinds of statements might go in the Conclusions section.) I think people will pay more attention to the Richmond University report than the Lawndale one.

To give your report the most impact, write your report like a newspaper story. Make the very first statement of your report (this will probably be the first statement of your executive summary) an interesting, intriguing one—like the lead sentence in a newspaper article. Write your headings like a newspaper headline. For example, use "Women Are Generally More Satisfied than Men" rather than "Differences Between Men and Women."

Keep it relevant. Focus on:

- Matters about which your readers can do something. Will anyone be able to use your finding that your college's students have an average of 1.2 siblings?

- Statistically significant differences. Don't tell your audience, for example, that 15% of your freshmen's mothers are teachers, compared with 16% of freshmen's mothers nationally.

    Keep in mind that a *statistically* significant difference may not be great enough to have *practical, meaningful* significance. Even though, in a

125

survey of 1500 freshmen, a 4% difference may be *statistically* significant, I tend to focus on and report only differences of, say, 10% or more. This focuses my audience on the *major* differences that warrant their attention.

- Interesting, unanticipated findings. Don't bother telling your readers, for example, that your Catholic students generally have Catholic parents, or that most of your full-time freshmen are 18 or 19 years old.

- Strengths, weaknesses, and recommendations.

Keep it short. Readership of a two-page report will be much higher than of a ten-page one. One institutional research office I know has a standing rule that none of its reports can be longer than one piece of paper. While I wouldn't make this a hard-and-fast rule, it's a good principle for ensuring that your efforts are paid attention to. If your report must be longer, include an easy-to-read executive summary that can be read and digested in no more than a minute or two.

Keep it organized. Use plenty of headings, so busy administrators and faculty can scan your report and read only what interests them.

Keep it simple. Even though your readers are well-educated, that doesn't mean they have the time or inclination to wade through dense prose. Just like you made it easy for your questionnaire readers to respond, use the suggestions below to make it easy for your report audience to understand what you're trying to tell them:

- ***Keep your sentences and paragraphs short.*** If one sentence runs four or five lines or one paragraph fills half a page, your report is too difficult to read.

- ***Spell out abbreviations*** at least the first time they are used, even if they are widely understood on your campus. Also spell out any numbers under 13.

- ***Use numbers sparingly***, only when they're necessary or inherently interesting. The "mathophobes" will glaze over a paragraph like the following:

   A greater percentage of Stetson College freshmen were first-generation college students than nationally. Exactly

40% of fathers and 48% of mothers had never attended college, compared to 37% and 40% of parents nationally. Over 36% of fathers of Stetson freshmen were college graduates, while nearly 27% of mothers had college degrees.

Now consider this rewrite:

The parents of Stetson College freshmen are not quite as well-educated as those of freshmen nationally; they are more likely to be simply high school graduates. Stetson freshmen are less likely to be going to college because their parents want them to.

Even though this paragraph has no figures, it communicates its point far more clearly. Often it's sufficient to say something is more or less, or above or below average, without getting into figures.

(The rewrite is also more effective because it is more succinct; the first sentence tells what the original paragraph took three sentences to say. Also note how the rewrite pulled a finding from another part of the survey to draw a connection about parents' education and their role in their children going to college.)

- **Round your figures** to the nearest whole number. People cannot digest more than two digits very easily and rarely care about greater accuracy than what's expressed in two digits. Few readers will care that 10.3% said X and 10.4% said Y; many will appreciate the increased readability of rounded statistics. To the "mathophobes" in your audience, overly precise statistics merely increase the number of figures they must examine. Unrounded numbers also encourage unsophisticated readers to focus on trivial, statistically insignificant differences.

- **Minimize citations.** Since this is not a scholarly paper, you need not include full citations, although you should of course explain in some less formal way the sources of any ideas that are not your own. You probably do not need to include a reference list or bibliography; anyone who would like a complete citation can contact you.

- **Have a friend read your draft.** Even if he or she knows no statistics, your friend should be able to follow the purpose of your study, your basic findings, and your conclusions and why you drew them.

Give your most important points visual impact. Desktop publishing techniques make it easy to achieve visual impact using these suggestions:

- Use larger fonts for headings and subheadings to draw attention to the statements you're using as headings.

- Put the headings along the left margin, making the margin wider than usual.

- Put the headings in a reverse font: white text on a black background.

- Use bulleted lists (like this one); readers can absorb them more quickly than a paragraph of text.

- Use "pull quotes": important statements taken from the body of the report and repeated in a larger, more readable typeface. They ensure that the major points of your report aren't missed.

For more ideas, look through any magazine you receive to see how it pulls you into an article and makes its point quickly.

These suggestions are not meant to imply that your report should have a casual tone. Your challenge is to keep it clear and simple while maintaining its dignity. Avoid slang, contractions, and undignified expressions ("really interesting"). Avoid writing in first person ("I," "we") or second person ("you"), although writing in the first person is increasingly acceptable if it streamlines and clarifies your report.

Keep it clear. Use plain English; avoid technical terms and research jargon such as "aggregate," "variable," "subject," or "population." Avoid formulas and statistical symbols; write "standard deviation" instead of "s," for example. Explain your statistics in everyday layperson's terms. It *is* possible, for example, to explain the results of regression analysis without ever using the term "regression," as shown in this example:

The main purpose of this report is to clarify the relation between SAT scores and high school rank and success at Snowden College. The report defines "success at Snowden" as an average grade of C during the freshman year.

The high school rank is by far the most important of the three measures—almost three times as important as the two SAT scores combined. The SAT Verbal score is the next most important. The SAT Math score is the least important; the contribution it makes is not even statistically significant.

High school rank and SAT scores account for about 11 percent of the variability in freshman grades. The remaining 89 percent could be explained by many other factors, including personality, background, maturity, and the kinds of courses taken in high school and at Snowden.

While the 11 percent figure seems low, it is probably typical of colleges similar to Snowden. Part of the reason it is low is because most of our students have very similar ranks and scores and students at each score or rank earn a wide range of grades. About two-thirds of our students, for example, score between 350 and 500 on the Verbal SAT, and their grades run the gamut from straight F's to straight A's. If we had many more students with weaker and stronger SATs and high school ranks, the relation between SAT scores and high school rank and freshman grades would look much stronger.

Make liberal use of simple tables and graphs. Many of your readers will be able to digest your main points more quickly from a simple table or graph than by wading through text. Spreadsheet or graphical software such as Microsoft Excel, Lotus, or Quattro Pro make it easy to prepare tables and graphs. Many word processing and desktop publishing packages include features for preparing effective tables.

How Can You Make Your Tables and Graphs Effective?

A picture is worth a thousand words only if it is a good one! Many tables and graphs are so poorly designed that they hinder rather than help understanding of the data. Here are some tips:

- *Give each table and graph a meaningful, self-explanatory title.* "Responses to Question 21" won't do it; "Freshman Self-Ratings of Academic Abilities" will.

- *Label every part of the table or graph clearly.* Label *each* table column and *each* graph axis. Avoid abbreviations and avoid writing labels vertically.

- *Make each table or graph self-explanatory*, since some readers will read tables or graphs without reading the text. Give definitions, assumptions, and notes in footnotes at the bottom of the table or graph.

- *Convert raw figures into percentages.* Few readers will care that 125 respondents agreed; more will care that only 23% did.

- *Make it easy for readers to hone in on differences and trends.* If your table is presenting results from this year's survey and last year's, add a third column computing the change. If your table is comparing men and women, add a third column computing the difference.

- *Avoid putting too much information into one table or graph.* If your pie chart has more than about five "slices," it is too detailed to make an impact. If you find you must insert vertical lines into your table to make it clear, you have too much data. Break your information into two or more tables, or simply delete some of it from your report. And don't forget to round your figures—at least to the nearest whole number!

- *Present your results in an order that makes sense to the reader* and helps convey your point. Many researchers tend to list results either in the order the questions were presented in the original questionnaire or in alphabetical order—orders that are rarely interesting or enlightening. Present checklist or multiple-choice results ranked with the most frequently chosen answers or highest ratings at the top, where the reader can quickly find them. (Appendix 7 gives an example.)

Keep in mind that people instinctively expect figures to grow larger as they move from left to right. Thus, when presenting trends over time, put the oldest data on the left and the most recent on the right.

- **Use the flexibility of modern spreadsheet, graphics, and presentation software packages to maximum effect.** Bar graphs, for example, need not have their bars drawn vertically; they might be more effective horizontally. Colors, fonts, and lines can be customized to make your point as clear as possible.

- **Draw attention to the point you want your table or graph to make.** Use boldface, italics, boxes, reverse font (white on black), or other highlights to draw attention to the most important figures. If you are comparing your institution against four peer institutions, put your institution's figures in boldface. Put totals in boldface, with details in normal font. In a survey asking about proposed changes to current policies, shade the bar representing current policy in a different color from the bars representing proposed changes. The reader can then quickly see how much support there is for change versus the status quo.

- **Consider using means or medians instead of totals.** Suppose you are showing the library budgets for your school and eight peers. A mean or median will be more informative to your readers than a total. Instead of placing the mean at the bottom of your table, list the nine institutions in order of budget size, and *insert the mean wherever it fits in* (using boldface and/or horizontal lines to help it stand out). This will allow your readers to quickly see which schools are above or below the mean. (Incidentally, an even more effective graph would show the budgets *per full-time-equivalent student* to minimize the impact of institutional size on the data.)

- **Don't assume a computer-generated table or graph is readable.** Some software generate distorted tables or graphs; some provide poor labels if any. If you prepare reports on surveys frequently, consider investing in good presentation/graphics software such as Aldus Persuasion, CorelDraw, Harvard Graphics, Microsoft PowerPoint, or

WordPerfect Presentations rather than relying on a spreadsheet package for your graphs and charts.

- **Date each graph and table and note its source.** Chances are good that they'll be pulled out of your report and shared separately.

Here is an example of a poor table from one school's results of the Cooperative Institutional Research Program's freshman survey:

Item	Stephens University			All Institutions			4 Yr Public Colleges		
	Male	Female	All	Male	Female	All	Male	Female	All
23. CHANCES ARE GOOD THAT STUDENTS WILL:									
Change majors	13.4%	13.2%	13.3%	11.7%	12.7%	12.2%	13.0%	13.4%	13.3%
Change Careers	10.9%	11.9%	11.5%	10.8%	12.8%	11.9%	11.4%	12.6%	12.1%
Get job in college	32.5%	42.1%	38.3%	35.2%	41.9%	38.8%	33.0%	41.1%	37.5%
Join frat. /sorority	14.8%	19.2%	17.5%	13.7%	17.2%	15.6%	17.3%	20.9%	19.3%
Play varsity athletics	29.0%	15.3%	20.7%	19.1%	9.9%	14.1%	22.3%	10.4%	15.6%
Make at least "B"s	39.3%	44.5%	42.4%	42.3%	44.3%	43.3%	40.8%	43.3%	42.2%
Graduate in 4 years	7.9%	8.3%	8.1%	8.3%	9.7%	9.0%	9.6%	10.3%	10.0%
Get B.A./B.S.	72.5%	81.1%	77.7%	63.7%	69.0%	66.6%	70.5%	76.1%	73.6%
Be satisfied with college	41.2%	55.2%	49.7%	44.2%	55.6%	50.4%	43.1%	53.2%	48.8%
Find a job in field	63.0%	68.2%	66.2%	63.3%	70.9%	67.4%	64.6%	71.2%	68.3%

Its flaws?

- There are too many columns of data—so many that vertical lines must be inserted to make them readable.

- The table tries to present too much information. One can use this table to compare men against women, the entire class against two sets of national averages, men against national averages for men, and women against two sets of national averages for women.

- The numbers are not rounded, so some readers will focus on trivial differences, such as 42.4% of Stephens freshmen expecting to make a "B" average, compared to 42.2% of freshmen at all four-year public colleges nationally.

- The table does not point out any meaningful differences. The reader must do the math to decide which differences are big and which aren't.

- The items aren't arranged in any particular order (beyond, perhaps, the order on the survey).

As a consequence of all these flaws, the table tells no story and has no apparent point. Few readers will derive anything meaningful from it.

Now compare the table above with the following revised version:

	Stephens College	Four-Year Public Colleges	Difference
23. Chances are good that student will. . .			
Find a job in major field	66%	68%	-2%
Be satisfied with college	50%	49%	+1%
Make at least a "B" average	42%	42%	—
Get a job in college	38%	38%	—
Play varsity athletics	21%	16%	+5%
Join fraternity or sorority	18%	19%	-1%
Change majors	13%	13%	—
Change careers	12%	12%	—
Take more than 4 yrs. to graduate	8%	10%	-2%

This table has a number of improvements:

- All the gender data have been eliminated, simplifying the table (if the author wants to make a point of gender differences, they can be put in a separate table).

- Only one rather than two sets of national norms is presented—the set that the author feels is of greatest interest.

- The survey items have been right-justified, so it is easy for the reader to read the correct figures for each item.

- All figures have been rounded to the nearest whole percentage, simplifying the table and encouraging readers to focus on more significant differences.

- The differences between the college's results and national norms have been computed and added in a new column.

- The items have been ordered from greatest agreement to least agreement.

All these changes make it much easier for the reader to discern the major stories the table is trying to tell: (1) Stephens students do not differ much from students nationally in their expectations, (2) most Stephens students are optimistic that they will find a job in their major field, and (3) few Stephens students expect to change their major or career plans. Of course, the text of the report should make these points, too. But, as noted earlier, many readers will skim the text and focus on the tables. This table helps those readers "get" the point that the author is trying to make.

Appendix 7 gives an example of a clear, simple report including tables.

When Should You Use a Graph Rather than a Table?

Deciding whether to present your findings with a table or a graph is an art. It depends, more than anything else, on the nature of your data and the story you are trying to tell.

Graphs are better than tables when you want to communicate your point quickly and dramatically, and when details such as precise figures are unimportant. They are particularly effective for showing relationships and trends. Most people find a well-done graph easier to understand and more interesting than a table; graphs are more likely to hold their attention.

Tables are better than graphs when you want to communicate exact figures and when you have a large number of figures to share. They are also more efficient: they can communicate a lot of information in a limited space. If you are under pressure to keep your report short, a table will probably allow you to share more than a graph. They are also easier to prepare than graphs; they can be well-done using any word processing software package, while an effective graph requires good spreadsheet or presentation graphics software (hand-drawn graphs are no longer acceptable in professional environments).

How Can You Make an Oral Presentation Interesting and Effective?

If you make an oral presentation, remember that even though you found your project fascinating in every detail, your audience probably won't. By keeping your remarks short and informal, concentrating on your findings, and allowing for questions, you will be able to home in quickly on the areas of major concern to your audience. (If they want to know more about how you did the survey, they'll ask.) A few handouts or overhead transparencies are essential, provided they are kept simple, uncluttered, and readable.

Here are some suggestions for making your overhead transparencies or slides most effective:

- Use the slide format that best meets your needs. To focus attention on key thoughts, use a bulleted list. To show trends and relative magnitude, use bar or line graphs. To show parts of a whole, use a pie chart. To show how parts are related, use a diagram.

- Use an outline to help you develop your bulleted slides. Your slides shouldn't repeat your remarks point-for-point. The text should be minimal, emphasizing only your *major* points. Don't let your slides be a crutch for your presentation.

- Limit the number of bullets per slide. Five or six are plenty, with no more than 15 total lines of text. Any more than that, and your audience will be trying to read it rather than listen to you, and your font will be too small to read anyway.

- Use a large font: 24-point for text and 36-point for major headings. Make sure that your projected slides can be read easily 50 feet away from the screen. Never, ever put 12-point text on slides for any reason!

- If your text, spreadsheet, or chart is too complex to present with a large font, share it through a handout rather than a slide.

- Round off all figures, as you did in your report.

- Invest in good presentation software such as Microsoft PowerPoint, Aldus Presentation, or WordPerfect Presentations. It will let you set up slides much more quickly and easily than many word processing or spreadsheet packages and will give you a wide selection of fonts, colors, and graphics.

- Use a color printer if one is available to make color transparencies, which will be much more interesting to your audience than black-and-white ones. If a color printer is unavailable, consider using a commercial service that will create color slides or transparencies from your diskette.

- Use an LCD panel and laptop computer if one is available. The panel is a unit wired to a laptop or other computer and placed on a high-intensity overhead projector. The panel shows the audience whatever is on the computer screen. It allows you to customize your presentation for each audience and use presentation effects such as graphics fades, dissolves, "building" effects (adding one bullet at a time), animation . . . even video and sound. Your audience will find your presentation much more appealing.

- If you are planning to use an LCD panel and laptop, a word of caution. Too many presentation effects (dissolves, builds, cartoons, colors) detract from your message, especially if your audience has a number of people who have never seen this kind of presentation before. A few months ago I made a presentation full of bells and whistles on an important proposal I was making to a group of VIPs. Afterwards many people commented on my great presentation, but not one commented on the substance of my proposal! LCD panels and laptops are not cheap, but they are coming down in price all the time. Another department at your institution may have ones you can borrow if you cannot afford one out of your budget. Or perhaps you could share the cost and the units with several departments.

You may wish to consider asking someone else to make the presentation or co-present it with you. Having someone viewed as important (say, a dean or vice president) make the presentation may help your study be taken more seriously. If you are uncomfortable with public speaking, asking a dynamic speaker to help with the presentation may make it more effective.

Postscript

Reacting to Other Surveys

Although the focus of this monograph has been on conducting your own survey, I hope that you will keep the points made here in mind when you are asked to complete other questionnaires or when you read reports on other surveys. A lot of surveys, both good and bad, are being done these days. We have a responsibility to support good surveys. Return the favors your respondents did for you by answering any good questionnaires you receive.

We have a similar responsibility to contravene bad surveys. Bad surveys hurt us. Past frustrations with them is one of the reasons that potential respondents refuse to help us. Bad surveys also waste the time we spend attempting to complete them, since the information gathered will be largely useless.

By refusing to cooperate with bad surveys, we not only stop wasting our time but may also contribute to a very low overall response rate. Perhaps that will make the researcher and his or her readers think twice about using the results or about conducting similar surveys in the future.

If you would like to discourage poor survey research, toss any questionnaire with any of the following characteristics right in the trash:

- No indication of who is sponsoring the survey.

- No explanation of how the results will be used.

- No guarantee of confidentiality.

- No clear definitions of ambiguous terms. (I once received a survey asking for "faculty workload" data . . . period. How many different definitions that term must have!) The person conducting the survey will end up with apples-and-oranges data that are useless.

- No postage-paid envelope in which to return the survey.

- A multi-page survey that will take a lot of time to complete (searching through files, calling other offices), unless the use to which it will be put clearly justifies the time.

- Any obviously biased or loaded questions. This includes requests for factual data that will obviously support only one side of an issue.

If you're nicer than I am, instead of throwing the questionnaire out, you might want to return the (uncompleted) survey with a brief note that you are unwilling to complete the survey because of its poor design but would consider completing a redesigned one.

We also have an obligation to critically review any reports on surveys before reacting to them or taking actions based on them. Any report you read should answer the following, or at least provide a contact to get the answers:

- *Who sponsored the survey?* Who paid for it? Why was it done? If someone with a vested interest in the results was the sponsor, the survey may be biased by biased questions, a biased sample, or a selective disclosure of the results.

- *When was the survey conducted?* Has anything happened in the interim that might change results if the survey were repeated today?

- *How were the people surveyed selected?* What evidence is there that they are an unbiased sample of the desired population?

- *How many people responded?*

- *What was the response rate?* What evidence is there that the respondents are a representative sample of the desired population?

- *How was the survey conducted*: by mail, by telephone, or in person?

- *What were the questions?* Small differences in wording can produce large differences in responses. The questions that produced the results should be quoted exactly.

- *In what order were the questions asked?* Sometimes questions asked early in the survey can influence later answers.

- *What is the error margin?*

- *What other research has been done on this topic?* Do these results corroborate or differ from other surveys or data?

- *Does the executive summary of the report accurately reflect the results*? The temptation to oversimplify or overreach for meaning is great.

I once worked for a short time as a radio announcer. When I was learning the ins-and-outs of radio, someone remarked to me, "Now that you know what we do, you'll never listen to radio the same way again." He was right; I will never again be able to listen as idly (or ignorantly) as I once did. I cannot help but be sensitive to what the announcer says, the "rotation" of the songs played, even the content and length of the commercials.

The story applies to survey research. Now that you know how to conduct a good survey, I hope you will never react in the same way to anyone else's questionnaire or report. Even if you never write another questionnaire yourself, our time will not have been wasted.

Appendix 1

AIR Code of Ethics

SECTION I: COMPETENCE.

I(a)   **Claims of Competence.** The institutional researcher shall not, in job application, resume, or the ordinary conduct of affairs, claim a degree of competency he/she does not possess.

I(b)   **Acceptance of Assignments.** The institutional researcher shall not accept assignments requiring competencies she/he does not have and for which she/he cannot effectively rely upon the assistance of colleagues, unless the supervisor has been adequately apprised.

I(c)   **Training of Subordinates.** The institutional researcher shall provide subordinates with opportunities for professional growth and development.

I(d)   **Professional Continuing Education.** The institutional researcher has the responsibility to develop her/his own professional skills, knowledge, and performance.

SECTION II: EXECUTION.

II(a)   **Use of Accepted Technical Standards.** The institutional researcher shall conduct all tasks in accordance with accepted technical standards.

II(b)   **Initial Discussions.** Before an assignment is begun, the institutional researcher shall clarify with the sponsor and/or major users the purposes, expectations, strategies, and limitations of the research.

        II(b)(I)   Special care shall be taken to recommend research techniques and designs that are appropriate to the purposes of the project.

        II(b)(ii)   Special care shall be taken to advise the sponsor and/or major users. Both at the design phase and, should the occasion arise, at any time during the execution of the project, if there is reason to believe that the strategy under consideration is likely to fail or to yield substantially unreliable results.

II(c)   **Identification of Responsibility.** The institutional researcher shall accept responsibility for the competent execution of all assignments which he/she, or a subordinate, undertakes, and shall display individual and/or office authorship, as appropriate, on all such reports.

II(d)   **Quality of Secondary Data.** The institutional researcher shall take reasonable steps to insure the accuracy of data gathered by other individuals, groups, offices, or agencies on which he/she relies, and shall document the sources and quality of such data.

II(e)   **Reports.** The institutional researcher shall ensure that all reports of projects are complete; are clearly written in language understandable to decision-makers; fully distinguish among assumptions, speculations, findings, and judgements; employ appropriate statistics and graphics; adequately describe the limitations of the project, of the analytical method, and of the findings; and follow scholarly norms in the attribution of ideas, methods, and expression and in the sources of data.

II(f)   **Documentation.** The institutional researcher shall document the sources of information and the process of analysis in each task in sufficient detail to enable a technically qualified colleague to understand what was done and to verify that the work meets all appropriate standards and expectations.

SECTION III: CONFIDENTIALITY.

III(a)   **Atmosphere of Confidentiality.** The institutional researcher shall establish a general atmosphere of awareness about confidentiality issues within the institutional research office.

III(b)   **Storage and Security.** The institutional researcher shall organize, store, maintain, and analyze data under his/her control in such a manner as to reasonably prevent loss, unauthorized access, or divulgence of confidential information.

III(c)   **Release of Confidential Information.** The institutional researcher shall permit no release of information about individual persons that has been guaranteed as confidential, to any person inside or outside the institution except in those circumstances in which not to do so would result in clear danger to the subject of the confidential material or to others; or unless directed by competent authority in conformity with a decree of a court of law.

III(d)   Special Standards for Data Collection.

III(d)(I)   **Balancing Privacy Risks Against Benefits.** The institutional researcher shall, at the design stage of any project, thoroughly explore the degree of invasion of privacy and the risks of breach of confidentiality that are involved in the project, weigh them against potential benefits, and make therefrom a recommendation as to whether the project should be executed, and under what conditions.

III(d)(ii)   **Developing Specific Guidelines.** The institutional researcher shall prepare or approve a written description of any specific steps beyond the regular guidelines within the institutional research office that are necessary during the execution of said assignment to insure the protection of aspects of privacy and confidentiality that may be at specific risk.

III(d)(iii)   **Disclosure of Rights.** The institutional researcher shall insure that all subjects are informed of their right of refusal and of the degree of confidentiality with which the material that they provide will be handled, including where appropriate, the implications of any freedom of information statute.

III(d)(iv)   **Apprisal of Implications.** The institutional researcher shall apprise institutional authorities of the implications and potentially binding obligations of any promise to respondents regarding confidentiality and shall obtain consent from such authorities where necessary.

SECTION IV: RELATIONSHIPS TO THE COMMUNITY.

IV(a)   **Equal treatment.** The institutional researcher shall promote equal access and opportunity regarding employment, services, and other activities of his/her office, without regard to race, creed, gender, national origin, disability or other accidental quality; and in analysis, demeanor, and expression shall be alert to the sensitivities of groups and individuals.

IV(b) **Development of Local Codes of Ethics.** The institutional researcher should develop and promulgate a code for ethics specific to the mission and tasks of the institutional research office; and should strive to cooperate with fellow practitioners in the mission in developing an institution-wide code of ethics governing activities in common.

IV(c) **Custody and Archiving.** The institutional researcher shall apply all reasonable means to prevent irrevocable loss of data and documentation during its immediately useful life; and, being aware of the role of data as institutional historic resource, shall act as advocate for its documentation and systematic permanent archiving.

IV(d) **Assessment of Institutional Research.** The institutional researcher shall develop and implement regular assessment tools for the evaluation of institutional research services.

IV(e) **Institutional Confidentiality.** The institutional researcher shall maintain in strict confidence and security all information in her/his possession about the institution or any of its constituent parts which by institutional policy is considered to be confidential, and shall pursue from Section III of this Code all processes for that purpose as are appropriate.

IV(f) **Integrity of Reports.** The institutional researcher shall make efforts to anticipate and prevent misunderstandings and misuse of reports within the institution by careful presentation and documentation in original reports, and by persistent follow-up contact with institutional users of those reports. If an institutional research report has been altered, intentionally or inadvertently, to the degree that its meaning has been substantially distorted, the institutional researcher shall make reasonable attempts to correct such distortions and/or to insist that institutional research authorship removed from the product.

IV(g) **External Reporting.** The institutional researcher has an obligation to the broader community to submit and/or report accurate data and professionally responsible interpretive material when requested by legitimate authority, including federal, state, and other governmental agencies and accrediting bodies. With respect to private inquiries, such as those from guidebook editors, journalists, or private individuals, the institutional researcher, should he/she respond, is bound by the same standards of accuracy and professionally responsible interpretation.

SECTION V: RELATIONSHIPS TO THE CRAFT.

V(a)   **Research Responsibilities.** The institutional researcher shall seek opportunities to contribute to participate in research on issues directly related to the craft and in other professional activities, and shall encourage and support other colleagues in such endeavors.

V(b)   **False Accusations.** Institutional researchers shall take care not to falsely demean the reputation or unjustly or unfairly criticize the work of other institutional researchers.

V(c)   **Unethical Conduct of Colleagues.** The institutional researcher shall take appropriate measures to discourage, prevent, or correct unethical conduct of colleagues when they are unwittingly or deliberately in violation of this code or of good general practice in institutional research.

Appendix 2

Sample Time Line for a Survey Research Project

Complete?	Task	Start date	Time needed	Deadline
_____	Plan survey.		2 weeks	
_____	Review what others have done.		2 weeks	
_____	Write questionnaire and cover letter.		1 week	
_____	Pilot-test questionnaire.		1 week	
_____	Design data analysis.		1 day	
_____	Arrange for data entry.		---	
_____	Write data analysis computer software.		1 week	
_____	Obtain mailing labels.		1 week	
_____	Select sample.		2 days	
_____	Collect additional data as needed.		2 weeks	
_____	Type and duplicate questionnaires, cover letters, and return envelopes.		2 weeks	
_____	Stuff envelopes for first mailing and mail.		2-3 days	
_____	Wait for returns.		2-3 weeks	
_____	Prepare follow-up mailing and mail.		2-3 days	
_____	Wait for returns.		2-3 days	
_____	Edit responses and begin data entry.		1-3 weeks	
_____	Analyze data.		2-3 days	
_____	Write report.		1 week	
_____	Have report typed and distributed.		1 week	

Note. These items need not be completed sequentially. For example, the data analysis can be designed and the mailing labels ordered while the questionnaires are being printed. Additional data can be collected while you are waiting for the questionnaires to be returned.

Appendix 3

Examples of Questionnaire Surveys Using Ecosystems

"WOMEN'S POWER" CONFERENCE

Please take a few minutes to give us your reactions to this year's conference. Your opinions will be very important to us as we plan our next conference.

Indicate your answers in the spaces provided. Feel free to add comments at the end of this form. Please drop this at the registration desk before you leave, or send to the address at the end of this form. Your response will be kept strictly confidential. Thank you very much for your help!

For items below, make two ratings: one on each session's quality and one on its usefulness to you. Leave blank any sessions you did not attend. Use the following rating scale:

        4 = very high
        3 = somewhat high
        2 = somewhat low
        1 = very low

	Quality	Usefulness to you
Thursday		
1. Commission on the Status of Women: System Network	____	____
2. Opening and Welcome	____	____
3. Changing Roles of Palestinian Women	____	____
4. Women in Leadership Roles in Manufacturing	____	____
5. Alternative Lifestyles: One Woman's Story	____	____
6. Women's Impact on the World	____	____
7. History of Women's Work in the United States	____	____
8. Women's Spirituality: Personal Stories	____	____
9. Keynote Speaker	____	____

	Quality	Usefulness to you
Friday		
10. Opening Remarks	___	___
11. Women and Nuclear Disarmament	___	___
12. Women and the Glass Ceiling	___	___
13. Women's Bodies and the Law	___	___
14. Women in U.S. Politics	___	___
15. Violence in Women's Lives	___	___
16. Closing Speaker	___	___
17. Commission on the Status of Women: Special Topics Discussion	___	___
18. Overall conference theme of Women's Power	___	___

This conference . . .	Strongly Agree	Agree	Disagree	Strongly Disagree
19. Helped me establish contacts with others who share me interests and concerns.	___	___	___	___
20. Addressed the latest developments in women's issues.	___	___	___	___
21. Gave me ideas on ways to handle personal and professional issues better.	___	___	___	___
22. Gave me ideas I will share with friends and colleagues.	___	___	___	___
23. Gave me renewed enthusiasm.	___	___	___	___

24. If you could have made one change in this year's conference, it would have been to:

_____

_____

_____

25. What should be the theme of next year's conference?

_____

_____

26. What special issues, topics, or tracks should be included in next year's conference programs? _____

_____

_____

27. Whom do you recommend we invite to speak at next year's conference?

NAME   TOPIC   HOW TO CONTACT

_____

_____

_____

28. How did you hear about this conference?
    _____ Brochure mailed to me
    _____ Newspaper ad
    _____ Newspaper article
    _____ Word of mouth
    _____ Other (please explain_____)

29. Which one of the following best describes you?
    _____ student
    _____ employee
    _____ Employed at another college or university
    _____ Employed elsewhere in the area
    _____ Full-time homemaker
    _____ Other (please explain _____)

30. Check all that apply:
    _____ Please add my name to the mailing list for next year's conference.
    _____ I would like to help plan and organize next year's conference.

                         Name _____
                         Address _____
                                 _____
                         Telephone _____

ADDITIONAL COMMENTS:

Thank you again for your help. Please drop this at the registration desk or mail to:

MERCYVILLE UNIVERSITY
TEACHER EDUCATION FOLLOW-UP SURVEY

Please complete this survey **even if you are not teaching**. Feel free to add comments at the end of this form. Thank you very much.

We would like to know how well you feel your course work at Mercyville has prepared you. For each skill, make <u>two</u> ratings: one on how <u>satisfied</u> you are with your preparation in that area, and one on how <u>important</u> it is to you to have sound preparation in that area. Use the following rating scale:

4 = very high
3 = somewhat high
2 = somewhat low
1 = very low

	Level of satisfaction	Importance to you
How well did your course work in EDUCATIONAL FOUNDATIONS prepare you in		
1. Professional teaching organizations?	____	____
2. School law (i.e., certification, students' rights, liability, teachers' rights)?	____	____
3. Current trends in education?	____	____
4. Typical school system structure?	____	____
5. Professional ethics?	____	____
6. Developing a personal philosophy of education?	____	____

7. ____ I did not take any Educational Foundations course work at Mercyville.

How well did your course work in EDUCATIONAL PSYCHOLOGY prepare you in

8. Theories of learning?	____	____
9. Measurement and evaluation techniques?	____	____
10. Child development?	____	____
11. Individual and cultural differences?	____	____
12. Models of teaching?	____	____

13. ____ I did not take any Educational Psychology course work at Mercyville.

	Level of satisfaction	Importance to you

How well did your training in INSTRUCTIONAL TECHNOLOGY components prepare you to

14. Use 2x2 slides, film, TV, programmed instruction, audio tape, transparencies, and other media to solve teaching-learning problems? _____ _____
15. Operate the school's TV and audiovisual equipment? _____ _____
16. Develop instructional media systems (i.e., interactive video, slide/tape, film, programmed instruction)? _____ _____
17. Evaluate the effectiveness of technology used in instruction? _____ _____
18. Locate sources of appropriate media materials? _____ _____
19. Produce appropriate instructional materials (i.e., 2x2 slides, transparencies, video and audio tapes, programmed instruction, slide/tapes)? _____ _____

20. _____ I did not receive any instruction in Instructional Technology components at Mercyville.

How well did your course work in MICROCOMPUTERS IN THE CLASSROOM prepare you to

21. Use a microcomputer for word processing? _____ _____
22. Evaluate microcomputer software? _____ _____
23. Use a microcomputer for classroom management? _____ _____
24. Integrate microcomputers into classroom instruction? _____ _____
25. Use microcomputers equitably in the classroom? _____ _____

26. _____ I did not take any Microcomputers in the Classroom course work at Mercyville.

BIG BROTHERS/BIG SISTERS OF GREATER LAWRENCE

BOARD MEMBERS SELF-ASSESSMENT

1. Please make two ratings of the attributes you bring to the Board: first, how much you can contribute in each capacity and, second, the agency's effectiveness in capitalizing on that capacity. Use the following scale:

    4 = Very high
    3 = Somewhat high
    2 = Satisfactory
    1 = Limited

How much you can contribute	How effectively the Board capitalizes	
____	____	Ability to give my time
____	____	Capacity to contribute financially
____	____	Contacts with Lancaster community leaders
____	____	Evaluation and assessment skills
____	____	Expertise with human services agencies
____	____	Financial management skills
____	____	Fund-raising skills
____	____	Knowledge of children and their needs
____	____	Knowledge of single-parent families and their needs
____	____	Legal skills
____	____	Marketing skills
____	____	Organizing skills
____	____	Personnel management skills
____	____	Strategic planning skills
____	____	Public relations skills
____	____	Public speaking skills
____	____	Volunteer training skills
____	____	Other skills or attributes (please describe:

_____

_____)

2. Please rate your understanding of agency activities using the following scale:

> 4 = Excellent
> 3 = Very good
> 2 = Satisfactory
> 1 = Unsatisfactory

_____ Agency policies
_____ Agency organization/chain of command
_____ Board organization/chain of command
_____ Agency's long-range plan or direction
_____ Agency's relationship with the United Way
_____ Agency's relationship with BBBS of America
_____ Agency's annual calendar and program time frame
_____ Agency's marketing/fund raising/public relations efforts
_____ Sources of agency funds
_____ Uses of agency funds
_____ Who our clients are
_____ Services we provide our clients
_____ Who our volunteers are
_____ Services we provide our volunteers
_____ Your role as a volunteer Board member of a non-profit agency
_____ Your specific, individual responsibilities
_____ Other Board members' interests and talents

3. Please make two ratings of your interactions with others associated with BBBS: first, your **satisfaction** with **how often** you have contact with each group and, second, your personal "comfort level" in working with each group. Use the following scale:

4 = Excellent
3 = Very good
2 = Satisfactory
1 = Unsatisfactory

Satisfaction with frequency of contact	Personal comfort level	
____	____	Other Board members on an individual basis
____	____	Other Board members as a group
____	____	Agency staff
____	____	Bigs and other volunteers
____	____	Littles

4. How well are your views and opinions respected by other Board members?
____ Extremely well respected
____ Very well respected
____ Somewhat well respected
____ Not well respected

5. Please rate your effectiveness as a Board member by circling the appropriate "grade," with A being outstanding and E being failing . . . just like your school days.

A B C D E	Attending Board meetings
A B C D E	Participating actively in Board meetings
A B C D E	Serving as an active committee member
A B C D E	Helping to establish policies
A B C D E	Learning about the agency
A B C D E	Understanding casework
A B C D E	Getting acquainted with other Board members
A B C D E	Getting acquainted with agency staff
A B C D E	Getting acquainted with Bigs and Littles
A B C D E	Working with volunteers and clients
A B C D E	Taking initiatives to help the agency
A B C D E	Volunteering to help where needed
A B C D E	Participating in fund-raising efforts
A B C D E	Serving as spokesperson for the agency
A B C D E	Contributing financially according to your means
A B C D E	Making sure your views are heard
A B C D E	Overall effectiveness

6. What have been your most significant personal accomplishments as a Board member? _____

_____
_____
_____

7. What additional contributions would you like to make that you have not made to date? _____

_____
_____

8. Additional comments (optional)

Appendix 4

Other Examples of Questionnaires

This appendix includes other examples of questionnaires written by the author.

OFFICE OF THE PRESIDENT
A_____ UNIVERSITY

SURVEY OF STUDENT GOALS AND SATISFACTION

Unless otherwise requested, check the <u>ONE</u> best response of each item. If you want to explain your answers further, use the space at the end of the questionnaire or attach another piece of paper.

1. What is your goal here at A_____ University?
    ____ To finish a degree here.
    ____ To prepare to transfer to another college before finishing a degree here.
    (What other college? _____)
    ____ At this time I'm not sure about my goal here.
    ____ Other (Please specify _____)

2. How would you describe A_____ to a friend back home? Check the part of each line that best shows your feelings.

Beautiful campus ___	___	___	___	___	Unattractive campus
Too expensive ___	___	___	___	___	Reasonably priced
Good academic reputation ___	___	___	___	___	Weak academic reputation
Good location ___	___	___	___	___	Poor location
Too big ___	___	___	___	___	Too small
Good financial aid ___	___	___	___	___	Little financial aid
Too close to home ___	___	___	___	___	Too far from home

3.   How would you describe A_____'s <u>courses</u> to a friend back home?
        Check the part of each line that best shows your feelings about the
        courses here <u>in general</u>.

                     Interesting ___ ___ ___ ___ ___ Boring
                  Usually closed ___ ___ ___ ___ ___ Easy to get into
          Conveniently scheduled ___ ___ ___ ___ ___ Inconveniently scheduled
                    Wide variety ___ ___ ___ ___ ___ Small selection
                            Easy ___ ___ ___ ___ ___ Hard
      Intellectually challenging ___ ___ ___ ___ ___ Mostly busy work

4.   How would you describe A_____'s <u>faculty</u> to a friend back home?
        Check the part of each line that best shows your feelings about the
        faculty here <u>in general</u>.

                 Cold and remote ___ ___ ___ ___ ___ Friendly
                Always available ___ ___ ___ ___ ___ Hard to find
                  Hard to talk to ___ ___ ___ ___ ___ Easy to talk to
                  Willing to help ___ ___ ___ ___ ___ Unwilling to help
             Hard to understand ___ ___ ___ ___ ___ Easy to understand
                    Enthusiastic ___ ___ ___ ___ ___ "Burned out"

5.   How would you describe your <u>academic advisor</u> to a friend back
        home? Check the part of each line that best shows your feelings.

                Always available ___ ___ ___ ___ ___ Hard to find
                  Hard to talk to ___ ___ ___ ___ ___ Easy to talk to
                  Willing to help ___ ___ ___ ___ ___ Unwilling to help
                 Cold and remote ___ ___ ___ ___ ___ Friendly
                Gives good advice ___ ___ ___ ___ ___ Gives poor advice

6.   How would you describe your <u>social life</u> at A_____ to a friend back
     home? Check the part of each line that best shows your feelings.

                  Nothing to do ___ ___ ___ ___ ___ Lots to do
              Hard to make friends ___ ___ ___ ___ ___ Easy to make friends
            Good athletics program ___ ___ ___ ___ ___ Weak athletics program
                   Poor facilities ___ ___ ___ ___ ___ Good facilities

7. Below are listed some opinions students sometimes express about college. Check all the statements that reflect your feelings.

___ A_____ University is a prestigious name in my community.
___ The program I'd like to major in here is not as good as I'd like.
___ I want to major in a program not offered here (What program?
_____)
___ I'm pretty good friends with a faculty member here.
___ I may have to leave A_____ because my grades aren't high enough.
___ I'm running into more financial problems than I expected when I came here.
___ I'd like to take a break from college for a year or so.
___ None of these statements applies to me.

8. What do you plan to major in?

_____

9. What one thing do you like best about A_____ University? Be specific!

10. What one thing about A_____ University most needs improvement? Be specific!

_____

Thank you very much for your help. Please return this questionnaire in the addressed, postage-paid envelope provided.

Today's date _____
Your guide's name _____
Your intended major _____

A_____ University
SUMMER ORIENTATION PROGRAM
STUDENT EVALUATION

We would like to know how successful the orientation program has been in familiarizing you with life at A_____ University. How worthwhile was each part of the orientation program? For each question, please check the space that best reflects your opinion. If you'd like to make any additional comments, please use the space at the end of this form. Thank you very much for your help.

How worthwhile was each of the following programs or presentations in acquainting you with A_____ and preparing you to attend here?

Program/presentation	Very Worthwhile	Somewhat Worthwhile	Not Worthwhile	Did Not Attend
First Day				
1. Welcomes from Orientation Committee and University administration	___	___	___	___
2. Placement and proficiency testing	___	___	___	___
3. Campus tour	___	___	___	___
4. "Somebody Else's Problem"	___	___	___	___
5. Intramurals	___	___	___	___
6. Resident Life	___	___	___	___
7. Commuter Life	___	___	___	___
8. Parent's Club (evening)	___	___	___	___
9. Student Guide and Video (evening)	___	___	___	___
10. Awareness workshop (evening)	___	___	___	___
11. Evening entertainment	___	___	___	___
Second Day				
12. Undecided/undeclared students	___	___	___	___
13. ROTC	___	___	___	___
14. Financial Aid	___	___	___	___
15. Library	___	___	___	___
16. Administrative Services	___	___	___	___
17. Student Affairs	___	___	___	___
18. Pre-registration academic advisement	___	___	___	___
19. Registration	___	___	___	___

For each of the following statements, please mark the space that best matches your feelings.

		Strongly Agree	Agree	Disagree	Strongly Disagree
20.	The check-in process went smoothly.	___	___	___	___
21.	My guide was knowledgeable.	___	___	___	___
22.	My guide was friendly.	___	___	___	___
23.	My guide was helpful.	___	___	___	___
24.	The food was good.	___	___	___	___
25.	The residence hall accommodations were clean and comfortable.	___	___	___	___
26.	The academic advisor I saw before registration was helpful.	___	___	___	___
27.	The registration process went smoothly.	___	___	___	___
28.	Overall, the presentations were easy to understand.	___	___	___	___
29.	Overall, the presentations were interesting.	___	___	___	___
30.	Overall, the people I met were helpful.	___	___	___	___
31.	Overall, these two days have been worthwhile.	___	___	___	___

32. What was the one best part of the entire program?

_____

_____

33. What one part of the program most needs improvement?

_____

_____

How does it need improvement? Be specific!

_____

_____

Additional comments:

Office of Institutional Research
B_____ College

Survey of Alumni Satisfaction, Activities, & Goals

Unless otherwise requested, <u>check the ONE best response</u> to each item. If you want to explain your answer further, use the space at the end of the questionnaire or attach another piece of paper.

1. If you could start over again, would you still go to college?
    _____   Yes, and I'd go to B_____
    _____   Yes, but I'd go somewhere else (Where? _____)
    _____   No.

2. How much did your education at B_____ contribute to your growth in your ability to:

	Very much	Somewhat	A little	Not at all
Define problems	___	___	___	___
Use a typical academic library	___	___	___	___
Understand others' ideas through reading	___	___	___	___
Understand others' ideas through listening	___	___	___	___
Appreciate how various fields of study are interrelated	___	___	___	___
Distinguish fact from opinion	___	___	___	___
Understand and appreciate different viewpoints on a given topic	___	___	___	___
Understand and apply scientific principles and methods	___	___	___	___
Use widely-accepted research techniques	___	___	___	___
Evaluate alternative solutions to a problem	___	___	___	___
Organize your ideas	___	___	___	___
Effectively explain your ideas orally	___	___	___	___
Effectively explain your ideas in writing	___	___	___	___
Perform basic computations	___	___	___	___
Appreciate the diversity of American culture	___	___	___	___
Appreciate other cultures	___	___	___	___

3. Since you graduated from B_____, have you participated in any of these activities ON YOUR OWN, <u>NOT</u> AS PART OF YOUR WORK OR SCHOOL ASSIGNMENTS? Check as many as apply.

_____ Browsed in a bookstore
_____ Had a library card
_____ Worked on a crossword or similar kind of puzzle
_____ Discussed a national or world news event with friends
_____ Attended an art museum or exhibit
_____ Read an article on scientific advances
_____ Attended a play or opera
_____ Set up a family budget
_____ Read a book dealing with a social or political issue
_____ Completed income tax forms on your own
_____ Read a "classic" literary work
_____ Attended a scientific exhibit

4. About how many hours per week do you read for leisure?
_____ hours per week

5. If you are presently employed, which of these do you need to do your job well? Check all that apply.

_____ I am not presently employed.
_____ Familiarity with methods of problem definition and solution
_____ Skill in critical thinking
_____ Ability to synthesize or merge knowledge from several sources
_____ Proficiency in your major field of study
_____ Acquaintance with other fields of study

Basic skills in:
_____ Reading
_____ Writing
_____ Speaking
_____ Computation

6. Have you ever applied for admission to one or more graduate degree programs?

_____ Yes, and I was accepted into at least one program.
_____ Yes, but I was never accepted.
_____ Yes, but I haven't heard from them yet.
_____ No.

7. What are the <u>highest</u> degrees beyond a Bachelor's that you've completed and that you plan to complete someday?

Have Completed	Plan to Complete	
___	___	None beyond a Bachelor's
___	___	Master's
___	___	Doctorate (Ph.D., Ed.D., etc.)
___	___	Professional degree (i.e., doctorate in medicine, law, or theology)
___	___	Other (Please specify _____)
___	___	I'm not sure.

8. Have you taken or do you plan to take any non-degree courses since graduating from B_____? Check all that apply.

	Have taken	Haven't taken but plan to
Adult education (non-credit)	___	___
Continuing Education (earning C.E.U. Credits)	___	___
College credit courses required to keep/advance my position at work	___	___
College credit courses for leisure	___	___

9. Based on your experience with B_____, what <u>one</u> thing about it most needs improvement? Be specific!

_____

_____

Thank you again for your help. Please return this questionnaire in the enclosed postage-paid envelope.

Appendix 5

Examples of Cover Letters

This appendix gives examples of cover letters. References to specific institutions have been deleted.

[letterhead paper]

Dear Student:

_____ University is committed to providing you with quality educational opportunities. One way to see if we are meeting our goals is to ask *you* how satisfied you are with _____'s various programs and features. Your input is very important in deciding what actions to take better to serve students who attend _____ and those who plan to come.

Your thoughts are particularly important in these critical times of budget cutbacks and uncertainties. Sharing your opinions and perceptions with us is perhaps the most valuable contribution you can make toward helping us address these problems and take action to solve them.

You are one of a small sample of students that was randomly selected to respond to a few questions on your goals and your satisfaction with _____. The small sample makes your response critical to the value of this study.

Would you please take a few minutes to complete the enclosed questionnaire? An addressed envelope (postage-paid if you live off campus) is included for you to return it. The number on the questionnaire will be used to contact and remind those not returning the questionnaire. Your name, of course, will never be connected with your individual answers.

If you have any questions about this study or if you would like a copy of the final report on it, please contact [name, title, address, telephone.]

Thank you for your help.

Sincerely,

[Name]
President

TO: All Board Members

FROM: Tom Smith, Chairperson
               Planning, Evaluation, & By Laws Committee

SUBJ: BOARD MEMBERS SELF-ASSESSMENT

Board policy stipulates that Board members shall conduct annual self-assessments of their individual effectiveness as board members. The purposes of the self-assessment are:

1.   To enable Board members to assess their own performance and decide privately what changes in their performance they should make; and

2.   To enable the Board to identify collective strengths and weaknesses of Board members and use this information in Board recruitment and Board development.

Enclosed is a copy of the instrument recently approved by the Board for that purpose. It will take you about ten minutes to complete.

After you have completed it, please return it to the agency office so the Board may use the aggregated results to plan ways to strengthen the Board. To keep your assessment confidential and make sure it is impossible for anyone to connect your name with your assessment, we have established the following process:

1.   Please seal your completed assessment in the smaller envelope marked "Board Self-Assessment."

2.   Place the sealed envelope in the larger envelope addressed to Vera Davis and mail or bring it to the agency office. Your name is on this larger envelope so Vera can note that you have completed the survey.

3.   When Vera receives your assessment, she will note that you have completed and returned it. She will then open the outer envelope only and discard it. She will then give the inner envelope, still sealed, to Dianne, who will open it in order to tabulate the responses.

Please contact me if you have any questions about this process. Thank you for participating in an activity that will enhance the Board and the agency.

Dear President _____:

Mr. John Smith, who last year served in my office as Presidential Intern (with the working title of Assistant to the President), is writing his dissertation to complete a doctorate in higher education at K_____ University. You may know his dissertation advisor, Dr. Steven Brown, President of Emeritus of K_____ University, due to his extensive involvement in AASCU. Dr. Brown is now teaching in the Graduate School of Education at K.U. and has been a close friend of mine for almost fifteen years.

I have mentored Mr. Smith along the way toward this degree because I value his work in my office and feel he will serve higher education with distinction in the future. As you know, I feel strongly about presidents mentoring potential leaders as an effective method of continuing the quality of leadership that we find within higher education today.

Mr. Smith has asked me for assistance in his dissertation research, and I am in turn asking for you to help him as well. His study explores the relationship between the leadership strategies used by university presidents and the collegiate culture, a subject which no doubt interests all presidents. Because no instrument exists to measure such a construct, Mr. Smith has developed his own questionnaire to gather the data. As you well know, researcher-developed questionnaires need to be examined by practitioners in the field. I am asking that you, as an expert in leading institutions of higher education, fill out his questionnaire . . . it should only take about fifteen minutes of your time. Because he needs not only your answers but your interpretation of the questions, Mr. Smith will call your office in the next week or two to conduct a short telephone interview or request an appointment for an on-site interview.

From one president to another, I am asking for your cooperation in this preliminary step as part of a significant study of higher education leadership, and on behalf of a fine young man with a bright future in the field.

Sincerely,

Michael Green
President

[letterhead paper]

Dear Graduate,

During the past year, my first year as President of Columbus College, I have enjoyed talking with current and former students to learn what you have to say about your experiences at Columbus.

Unfortunately, it is impossible for me to talk with all of you face-to-face.

So that I may have the benefits of your insights into what the College is doing right—and where the College can improve—I ask that you take about ten minutes to complete and return the survey enclosed with this letter. In essence, by participating in this survey, you will be advising me on the direction and thrust of future changes at the College. Your responses will be completely confidential. (The identification number on the survey is to help us compile mailing statistics.)

I look forward to receiving your survey responses. If you have any questions or concerns about the questionnaire, please contact the Office of Institutional Planning and Assessment, [address], or call [telephone number].

Sincerely,

Warren Peterson, Ph.D.
President

Appendix 6

Example of Telephone Survey Interviewer Guidelines

Interviewer Tasks

1. Be familiar with the questionnaire. Fill out one for yourself before you start calling others (if you like, you can hand it in with your completed surveys).

2. Make your calls between Sunday, September 25, and Saturday, October 1.

3. The best time to call is between 6:30 and 9 p.m. A rainy evening would be especially good. Don't call after 9:15 p.m. or before 9 a.m.

4. Review your instructions before you begin.

5. Be casual, conversational, and friendly. Avoid both an "over-rapport" and an overly "mechanical" interviewing style. Don't be too friendly, but don't be too "unfriendly" either.

6. Read the questions precisely, as written, in the order given. It is extremely important that everyone be asked the same question in the same way. Even a difference in one word could drastically change the meaning and, thus, the response. Do *not* try to interpret the questions in your own words.

7. Repeat answers for the person if there is any doubt.

8. Ask *all* the questions unless otherwise indicated in the instructions.

9. Record responses carefully and legibly.

10. Double check the completed questionnaire. Make sure all answers are clearly marked and all written comments are legible.

11. We must have every person in the sample accounted for in some way. Record *every* call you make, even if the number is not working, you get a wrong number, there was no answer, or the interview was not completed. Feel free to record any pertinent comments on the front page of the survey.

12. Don't smoke, eat, or drink while conducting the interview. You have too much to concentrate on without having to worry about dropping or spilling something.

Staying Neutral

We want every question to mean the same thing to every person we call. Therefore, please try to stay *neutral* as you conduct each survey.

Neutral responses are difficult for most of us, since in normal phone behavior we often try to convince the other person of something—date, meeting, what to do, etc. We are usually not neutral but advocates.

Telephone interviewing calls for us to drop this persuasive tactic, except when introducing the interview. It is then and only then that we use our powers of persuasion to get a prospective respondent to agree to an interview.

1. Be an "active" listener, but only give the minimum of reinforcement, such as "OK," "I see," or "uh huh."

2. Avoid any unnecessary or overly enthusiastic reinforcement, such as "Wonderful!" or "Boy, you've got that right."

3. Don't give the respondent your own opinion.

Confidentiality

The only way we can be successful is to establish and maintain a reputation for confidentiality. Therefore, please:

1. Do not tell anyone the names of the people you have been asked to call.

2. Do not tell anyone the substance of any call or any part of a call, no matter how fascinating or funny it was.

3. Please don't talk about your summary of findings. Just because 90 percent of your respondents gave a certain opinion doesn't meant that 90 percent of all the other respondents felt that way. And the people you tell may tell others, who may then question the figures in our final report.

HOW TO HANDLE PROBLEMS

Most people like to talk about themselves and what they know. Once their initial anxieties are relieved, most people you call will participate in the survey because of this fact and the guarantee of a good listener—you.

IF THE NUMBER IS BUSY OR NOT WORKING OR THERE IS NO ANSWER:

Let the phone ring 4 or 5 times before hanging up.

Dial the number one more time to be sure you can't get through.

Try a busy number again about 30 minutes later.

IF YOU REACH AN ANSWERING MACHINE

Say something like "Hello, I am calling for Manor School District. We're conducting a survey of Manor residents about their views on Manor schools. I'll try to contact you again later." If you like, leave your name and phone number.

IF THE PERSON YOU ARE CALLING FOR IS UNABLE OR UNWILLING TO COOPERATE:

Try to get another adult member of that household.

IF THE PERSON HESITATES AFTER YOU ASK HIS OR HER CONSENT:

Do some *prodding*:

> "This won't take much time and we really do want your opinion."

> "Since your name was drawn, we need to talk to you in order for our survey to be a true representation of the community."

> "Let me remind you that your responses will be confidential."

IF THE RESPONDENT MAKES COMMENTS:

If they seem relevant to the questions, try to write them down in the margins.

IF THE RESPONDENT IS UNCLEAR ABOUT THE QUESTIONS YOU READ:

Do *not* try to interpret the questions in your own words. Say:

> "This is all the information available to me."

> "We would like you to answer the question the way it is written. Could I read it for you again?"

> "I'm sorry, but I don't have that information."

> "I will write on the questionnaire the qualifications to your answer you just mentioned."

IF YOU'RE UNSURE OF A RESPONDENT'S FINAL ANSWER

Repeat what you think it is so he or she can confirm or correct it.

IF THE RESPONDENT GIVES SOMEONE ELSE'S OPINION

Everything should be in terms of what the *respondent* thinks--not the respondent's children, spouse, neighbors, etc. Therefore, you might need to say:

> "I see. Now, is that what *you* think?"

> "It's *your* opinion we really want."

IF THE RESPONDENT HESITATES ON THE OPEN-ENDED QUESTIONS (42 AND 43):

Try to *coax* him or her:

> "Is there anything you'd like to say?"

> "Are you sure you don't want to answer?"

Be careful about leading the respondent. Probes should be *neutral* requests for information.

IF A PERSON BECOMES IRATE, USES FOUL LANGUAGE, GOES ON A TIRADE, ETC.:

Be nice! Do not hang up. Possible responses:

"Yes, I see."

"Uh huh."

"Yes, I understand you feel quite strongly about this matter."

"Let me repeat the question for you, sir."

Do *not*, under any condition, *argue, insert your own opinion, or, worst of all, lose your temper.*

Try to continue the interview unless the respondent refuses to answer.

If all else fails, wait for an opportunity to speak, then say something like:

"I'm awfully sorry you prefer not to complete the interview, but thank you anyway. Goodbye, Mr./Mrs. _____."

IF YOU HAVE ANY QUESTIONS OR PROBLEMS:

Call Mrs. Joan Smith, 555-1234 between 8:00 a.m. and 4:30 p.m. If she is not there, leave a message (say you are with the Manor survey) and she will get back to you as soon as she can.

Dear Manor School District Resident,

You were recently selected from either student records or tax records to participate in a survey to find out your opinions regarding the Manor School District. During the week of September 26-30, an interviewer will telephone you to conduct a five minute survey. All of your answers and comments will be confidential and your participation is completely voluntary. As a district resident your input is very important to us, and we would greatly appreciate your assistance. If you have any questions about this survey, please call Mr. Mark Stewart at 555-4321.

Charles Blakeley
Superintendent

Respondent Name _____

Phone No. _____

Note when you couldn't get through:

Date	Time	Busy/No Answer?
_____	_____	_____
_____	_____	_____
_____	_____	_____
_____	_____	_____

MANOR SCHOOL DISTRICT INTERVIEW

Hello, could I speak to _____ ?

> IF WRONG NUMBER: I'm sorry to have bothered you.

> IF NOT IN: When would be a good time to reach him/her?

This is _____ calling from Manor School District. We're conducting a survey of Manor residents about their views on schools.

A few days ago a postcard describing the survey was sent to you. Did you receive it?   YES   NO

> IF NO: I'm sorry it didn't reach you. The postcard was to tell you about this call and the purpose of the survey.

We're contacting parents and taxpayers to find out how satisfied you are with Manor schools. Even if you do not presently have children in Manor schools, as a taxpayer your input is very important in deciding how the school district can improve its services and programs.

Your name was picked at random, and your responses will be kept strictly confidential.

1. The interview will take about five minutes. Please feel free to ask questions at any time and you may refuse to answer any question if your wish. There will be a chance to make comments at the end of the survey. Okay?
    OKAY   REFUSED

First, Manor school district is considering expanding some of its programs and services. This might, of course, mean higher taxes to pay for them. For each item I read, please tell me Yes if you feel more money should be spent to do it, No if you do not feel more money should be spent, or Maybe if you're not sure.

2.	Expanding drug and alcohol prevention programs	YES	NO	MAYBE
3.	Preventing drop outs	YES	NO	MAYBE
4.	Improving school buildings and equipment	YES	NO	MAYBE
5.	Improving athletic buildings and fields	YES	NO	MAYBE
6.	Increasing computer instruction	YES	NO	MAYBE
7.	Increasing vocational training	YES	NO	MAYBE
8.	Increasing adult education programs	YES	NO	MAYBE
9.	Providing recreational programs for community residents	YES	NO	MAYBE
10.	Improving bus services	YES	NO	MAYBE
11.	Increasing after-school programs for children whose parents work	YES	NO	MAYBE
12.	Providing programs for pre-schoolers aged 2 to 5	YES	NO	MAYBE
13.	Increasing teachers' salaries	YES	NO	MAYBE
14.	Making classes smaller	YES	NO	MAYBE

Now we'd like to know how successfully you think the school district is meeting its goals. For each item I read, please respond Excellent, Good, Fair, Poor, or tell me if you have no opinion.

15.	Developing basic skills in reading, writing, and mathematics	Exc	Good	Fair	Poor	NoOpin
16.	Developing good work habits in students	Exc	Good	Fair	Poor	NoOpin

17. Preparing responsible citizens	Exc	Good	Fair	Poor	NoOpin
18. Providing academic counseling	Exc	Good	Fair	Poor	NoOpin
19. Challenging gifted and talented students	Exc	Good	Fair	Poor	NoOpin
20. Preparing students for careers in vocational-technical subjects	Exc	Good	Fair	Poor	NoOpin
21. Preparing students for careers in agriculture	Exc	Good	Fair	Poor	NoOpin
22. Preparing student for college	Exc	Good	Fair	Poor	NoOpin
23. Providing extracurricular sports programs	Exc	Good	Fair	Poor	NoOpin
24. Providing extracurricular programs in music, theater, and art	Exc	Good	Fair	Poor	NoOpin
25. Maintaining high standards students	Exc	Good	Fair	Poor	NoOpin
26. Making sure all teachers are capable and professional	Exc	Good	Fair	Poor	NoOpin
27. Maintaining well-kept, modern buildings and classrooms	Exc	Good	Fair	Poor	NoOpin
28. Dealing with growth and overcrowding	Exc	Good	Fair	Poor	NoOpin
29. Controlling its budget	Exc	Good	Fair	Poor	NoOpin
30. Communicating with the community	Exc	Good	Fair	Poor	NoOpin
31. Disciplining students	Exc	Good	Fair	Poor	NoOpin

32. Manor offers adult education courses after school hours so adults can improve their skills and learn more about things that interest them. Do you think you might be interested in taking such courses?   YES   NO

IF NO: Go to question 44.

IF YES: I'm going to read you a list of courses that Manor is considering offering. For each course, if you'd be interested in taking it please say Yes, if you'd definitely not be interested, please say No, and say Maybe if you're unsure.

33. Recreation and gym activities   YES   NO   MAYBE

   IF RESPONDENT HESITATES: Please respond Yes if you're interested, No if you're not interested, or Maybe if you're not sure.

34. Aerobics and other fitness programs   YES   NO   MAYBE

35. Computer or word processing training   YES   NO   MAYBE

36. Arts and crafts   YES   NO   MAYBE

37. How to make and finish home furnishings YES   NO   MAYBE

38. Personal finances and taxes   YES   NO   MAYBE

39. Typing and other office skills   YES   NO   MAYBE

40. Parenting and child care   YES   NO   MAYBE

41. Sewing or cooking   YES   NO   MAYBE

42. In your own words, what would you say is the greatest strength of Manor schools?
    (IF BROAD: Could you be more specific?)
    (IF LONG ANSWER: Please excuse me while I write down your answer.)

_____

_____

43. In your own words, what one thing about Manor schools most needs improvement?
    (IF BROAD: Could you be more specific?)
    (IF LONG ANSWER: Please excuse me while I write down your answer.)

_____

_____

44. Now just a few last, quick questions. How many years have you lived in Manor District? _____

Do you have any children in Manor schools?   YES   NO

IF YES: How Many?   _____

45. - 51   What grades are they in?   _____
                (WRITE DOWN A GRADE FOR *EACH* CHILD)

IF NO: 52. Have you ever had children in Manor Schools?   YES   NO

This concludes the survey. Thank you very much for your time, and I hope you have a pleasant evening.

Example of a Summary Report of a Questionnaire Survey

Big Brothers/Big Sisters of Greater Lawrence
Summary of Board Members Self-Assessment

How Much Board Members Can Contribute (Question 1)

As a whole, Board members rated themselves at least satisfactory in all respects; there are no obvious weaknesses among Board members collectively.

Board members rated themselves particularly high in

> Organizing skills;
> Evaluation and assessment skills;

so these are not skills we need to look for in potential new board members.

Board members rated themselves lowest (although still "Satisfactory on average) in legal skills.

How Effectively the Board Capitalizes on Member Capabilities (Question 1)

As a whole, Board members felt the Board capitalizes on them at least satisfactorily in most respects.

Board members felt the Board capitalized best on their

> Ability to give time;
> Capacity to contribute financially.

Board members felt the Board capitalized to only a limited extent on their volunteer training skills. Perhaps better means of capitalizing on these skills could be explored.

Difference Between Potential and Capitalization (Question 1)

When compared to their ability to contribute, Board members felt the Board was doing the best job capitalizing on their

> Capacity to contribute financially;
> Ability to give time;
> Fund-raising skills.

Board members felt the Board was relatively less effective capitalizing on their

> Public speaking skills;
> Public relations skills;
> Organizing skills;
> Volunteer training skills.

Perhaps better means of capitalizing on these skills could be explored.

Understanding Agency Activities (Question 2)

As a whole, Board members rated themselves at least satisfactory in all respects in their understanding on agency activities. There are no obvious weaknesses among Board members collectively in this regard.

Board members rated themselves highest in their understanding of

> Agency organization/chain of command;
> Board organization/chain of command;
> Role as a volunteer Board member of a non-profit agency;
> Specific, individual responsibilities.

Board members rated themselves only satisfactory on average in their understanding of

> Agency's relationship with BBBS of America;
> Services we provide our volunteers;
> Other Board members' interests and talents.

Perhaps these could be the focus of future Board development activities.

179

Interactions with Others Associated with BB/BS (Question 3)

As a whole, Board members rated themselves at least satisfactory in their satisfaction with frequency of contact with all BB/BS cohorts. There is no obvious dissatisfaction among Board members collectively in this regard.

Board members rated themselves only satisfactory on average in their satisfaction with frequency of contact with

Littles;
Bigs and other volunteers.

Perhaps new avenues for increasing contact with these groups could be explored.

How Well Views and Opinions are Respected by Other Board Members (Question 4)

All Board members felt their views and opinions are at least somewhat well respected by other Board members. Over two-thirds felt their views and opinions are very well or extremely well respected.

Effectiveness as a Board Members (Question 5)

Board members gave themselves an average of "B" in their effectiveness in most respects.

Board members gave themselves the highest average ratings on

Attending Board meetings;
Learning about the agency.

They gave themselves an average of "C" in

Understanding casework;
Serving as spokesperson for the agency;
Getting acquainted with Bigs and Littles.

They gave themselves an average of "D" in

Working with volunteers and clients.

Perhaps avenues for helping Board members strengthen themselves in these respects could be explored.

Conclusions

Board members are, on the whole, an effective group. There are, however, a few areas that could be strengthened:

1.　　When recruiting new Board members, it might be helpful to look for those with legal skills.

2.　　Board members have "hidden talents" in

>　Organizing;
>　Volunteer training;
>　Public relations;
>　Public speaking;

that should be better capitalized by the agency. They would appreciate training that would enable them to serve as spokespeople for the agency.

3.　　Board members would benefit from development activities that strengthen their understanding of the agency's relationship with BBBS of America and help them learn about the interests and talents of other Board members.

4.　　Board members would benefit from development activities that would strengthen their familiarity with and understanding of the agency's principal activity: casework with Bigs and Littles. In particular, they would benefit from more information on casework and other services we provide and from opportunities to get acquainted and work with Bigs and Littles.

Question 1, ordered by how much Board members can contribute

		How much you can contribute	How effectively Board capitalizes	Difference
Organizing skills	**Somewhat high**	3.1	2.5	-0.6
Evaluation and assessment skills	**Somewhat high**	2.8	2.5	-0.3
Knowledge of children and their needs	**Somewhat high**	2.5	2.2	-0.3
Public relations skills	**Somewhat high**	2.5	1.8	-0.7
Strategic planning skills	**Somewhat high**	2.5	2.4	-0.1
Ability to give my time	**Satisfactory**	2.4	3.0	0.6
Financial management skills	**Satisfactory**	2.4	2.7	0.3
Public speaking skills	**Satisfactory**	2.4	1.5	-0.9
Personnel management skills	**Satisfactory**	2.4	2.1	-0.3
Knowledge of single-parent families and their needs	**Satisfactory**	2.2	2.2	0.0
Marketing skills	**Satisfactory**	2.1	2.0	-0.1
Contacts with Lawrence community leaders	**Satisfactory**	2.1	2.5	0.4
Capacity to contribute financially	**Satisfactory**	2.0	2.9	0.9
Expertise with human services agencies	**Satisfactory**	1.9	2.3	0.4
Legal skills	**Satisfactory**	1.5	1.8	0.3
Volunteer training skills	**Limited**	1.9	1.5	-0.4

Question 1, ordered by how effectively Board capitalizes on member capabilities:

		How much you can contribute	How effectively Board capitalizes	Difference
Ability to give my time	**Somewhat high**	2.4	3.0	0.6
Capacity to contribute financially	**Somewhat high**	2.0	2.9	0.9
Financial management skills	**Somewhat high**	2.4	2.7	0.3
Evaluation and assessment skills	**Somewhat high**	2.8	2.5	-0.3
Fund-raising skills	**Somewhat high**	2.1	2.5	0.4
Organizing skills	**Somewhat high**	3.1	2.5	-0.6
Contacts with Lawrence community leaders	**Satisfactory**	2.1	2.5	0.4
Strategic planning skills	**Satisfactory**	2.5	2.4	-0.1
Expertise with human services agencies	**Satisfactory**	1.9	2.3	0.4
Knowledge of children and their needs	**Satisfactory**	2.5	2.2	-0.3
Knowledge of single-parent families and their needs	**Satisfactory**	2.2	2.2	0.0
Personnel management skills	**Satisfactory**	2.3	2.1	-0.3
Marketing skills	**Satisfactory**	2.1	2.0	-0.1
Public relations skills	**Satisfactory**	2.5	1.8	-0.7
Legal skills	**Satisfactory**	1.5	1.8	0.3
Public speaking skills	**Satisfactory**	2.4	1.5	-0.9
Volunteer training skills	**Limited**	1.9	1.5	-0.4

Question 1, ordered by difference between potential and capitalization:

	How much you can contribute	How effectively Board capitalizes	Difference	
Capacity to contribute financially	2.0	2.9	0.9	Board Overcapitalizes
Ability to give my time	2.4	3.0	0.6	
Fund-raising skills	2.1	2.5	0.4	
Contacts with Lawrence community leaders	2.1	2.5	0.4	
Expertise with human services agencies	1.9	2.3	0.4	
Financial management skills	2.4	2.7	0.3	
Legal skills	1.5	1.8	0.3	
Knowledge of single-parent families and their needs	2.2	2.2	0.0	
Strategic planning skills	2.5	2.4	-0.1	
Marketing skills	2.1	2.0	-0.1	
Personnel management skills	2.4	2.1	-0.3	
Evaluation and assessment skills	2.8	2.5	-0.3	
Knowledge of children and their needs	2.5	2.2	-0.3	
Volunteer training skills	1.9	1.5	-0.4	
Organizing skills	3.1	2.5	-0.6	
Public relations skills	2.5	1.8	-0.7	
Public speaking skills	2.4	1.5	-0.9	Board Undercapitalizes

For More Information

Below are listed print, electronic, and organizational resources for further information on the various aspects of survey research. The print resources are grouped by topic. A very extensive, annotated bibliography (nearly 500 sources) is in Berdie et al.'s *Questionnaires: Design and use* (listed below). A 15-page glossary of terms relevant to the design, administration, and analysis of surveys is in Babbie's *Survey research methods* (also listed below).

General References on Survey Research and Questionnaire Design

Babbie, E. (1990). *Survey research methods* (2nd ed.). Belmont, CA: Wadsworth Publishing Co., Inc.

Backstrom, Charles H., & Hursh-Cesar, Gerald. (1981). *Survey research* (2nd ed.). New York: Wiley & Sons.

Berdie, D., Anderson, J., & Niebuhr, M. (1986). *Questionnaires: Design and use* (2nd ed.). Metuchen, NJ: Scarecrow Press.

Bradburn, Norman M., & Sudman, Seymour. (1979). *Improving interview method and questionnaire design*. San Francisco: Jossey-Bass.

Bradburn, Norman M., & Sudman, Seymour. (1988). *Polls and surveys: Understanding what they tell us*. San Francisco: Jossey-Bass.

Bourque, Linda B., & Fielder, Eve P. (1995). *How to conduct self-administered and mail surveys*. Thousand Oaks, CA: Sage Publications.

Converse, J. M., & Presser, S. (1986). *Survey questions: Handcrafting the standardized questionnaire*. Newbury Park, CA: Sage Publications.

deVaus, D. (1990). *Surveys in social research* (2nd ed.). London: Unwin Hyman.

Dillman, Donald. (1976). *Mail and telephone data collection methods*. New York: Wiley-Interscience.

Dillman, Donald. (1978). *Mail and telephone surveys: The total design method*. New York: John Wiley & Sons.

Erdos, P. (1970). *Professional mail surveys.* New York: McGraw-Hill.

Ferber, R. (Ed.). (1974). *The handbook of marketing research.* New York: McGraw-Hill.

Fink, Arlene. (1995). *A survey handbook.* Thousand Oaks, CA: Sage Publications.

Fink, Arlene. (1995). *How to ask survey questions.* Thousand Oaks, CA: Sage Publications.

Fink, Arlene. (1995). *How to design surveys.* Thousand Oaks, CA: Sage Publications.

Fink, Arlene, & Kosecoff, Jacqueline. (1985). *How to conduct surveys: A step by step guide.* Thousand Oaks: Sage Publications.

Fowler, Floyd J., Jr. (1993). *Survey research methods* (2nd ed.). Thousand Oaks, CA: Sage Publications.

Gray, R., Jacobson, E., Micek, S., Patrick, C. Renkiewicz, N., & Van Dusen, W. (1979). *Student outcomes questionnaires: An implementation handbook.* Boulder, CO: National Center for Higher Education Management Systems and the College Board.

Henerson, M., Morris, L. & Fitz-Gibbon, C. (1987). *How to measure attitudes.* Newbury Park: Sage Publications.

Labaw, P. (1980). *Advanced questionnaire design.* New York: Harper Business, Inc.

Lees-Haley, P. (1980). *The questionnaire design handbook.* Huntsville, AL: Rubicon.

Lindemann, W. (1983). *Attitude and opinion research: Why you need it/how to do it* (3rd ed.). Washington, DC: Council for Advancement and Support of Education.

Lockhart, D. (Ed.). (1984). *Making effective use of mailed questionnaires.* (New Directions for Program Evaluation Serial No. 21). San Francisco: Jossey-Bass.

Mangione, Thomas W. (1995). *Mail surveys: Improving the quality.* Thousand Oaks, CA: Sage Publications.

McKenna, B. (Ed.). (1983). *Surveying your alumni: Guidelines and 22 sample questionnaires.* Washington, DC: Council for Advancement and Support of Education.

Oppenheim, A. (1966). *Questionnaire design and attitude measurement.* New York: Basic Books.

Payne, S. (1951). *The art of asking questions.* Princeton, NJ: Princeton University Press.

Rossi, Peter Henry, Wright, James D., & Anderson, Andy B. (Eds.). (1983). *Handbook of survey research.* New York: Academic Press.

Salant, Priscilla, & Dillman, Don. (1994). *How to conduct your own survey.* New York: John Wiley & Sons.

Schuman, H., & Presser, S. (1981). *Questions and answers in attitude surveys.* New York: Academic Press.

Sudman, Seymour, & Bradburn, Norman M. (1982). *Asking questions: A practical guide to questionnaire design.* San Francisco: Jossey-Bass.

Other Important References on Questionnaires and Survey Design

Adams, L. & Gale, D. (1982). Solving the quandary between questionnaire length and response rate in educational research. *Research in Higher Education, 17*(3), 231-240.

Aiken, Lewis R. (1988). The problem of nonresponse in survey research. *Journal of Experimental Education, 56*(3), 116-119.

Alwin, Duane F. (1977). Making errors in surveys: An overview. *Sociological Methods and Research, 6*(2), 131-150.

Anderson, J. (1986, April). *Questionnaire design and use revisited: Recent developments and issues in survey research.* Paper presented at the Annual Meeting of the American Educational Research Association, San Francisco.

Angleitner, Alois, & Wiggins, Jerry S.(Eds.). (1986). *Personality assessment via questionnaires: Current issues in measurement and theory.* Berlin: Springler-Verlag.

Boser, Judith A. (1990). Surveying alumni by mail: Effect of booklet/folder questionnaire format and style of type on response rate. *Research in Higher Education, 31*(2), 149-159.

Boser, Judith A., & Clark, Sheldon B. (1993). *Response rates in mail surveys: A review of the reviews.* (ERIC Document Reproduction Service No. 356 278)

Bourque, Linda B., & Clark, Virginia A. (1992). *Processing data: The survey example.* Thousand Oaks, CA: Sage Publications.

Bradburn, Norman M., Sudman, Seymour, and Associates. (1979). *Improving interview method and questionnaire design: Response effects to threatening questions in survey research.* San Francisco: Jossey-Bass.

Brehm, John. (1993). *The phantom respondents: Opinion surveys and political representation.* Ann Arbor: University of Michigan Press.

Brennan, Mike. (1992). Techniques for improving mail survey response rates. *Marketing Bulletin, 3,* 24-27.

Carifio, James, Biron, Ronald, & Shwedel, Allen. (1991). A comparison of community college responders and nonresponders to the VEDS student follow-up survey. *Research in Higher Education, 32*(4), 469-477.

Childers, D. & Ferrell, C. (1979). Response rates and perceived questionnaire length in mail surveys. *Journal of Marketing Research, 16*(3), 429-431.

Converse, Jean M., & Presser, Stanley. (1986). *Survey questions: Handcrafting the standardized questionnaire.* Newbury Park, CA: Sage Publications.

Cote, Lawrence S., et al. (1986). Increasing response rates to mail surveys: The impact of adherence to Dillman-like procedures and techniques. *Review of Higher Education, 9*(2), 229-242.

Denton, Jon J., et al. (1988). Effects on survey responses of subjects, incentives, and multiple mailings. *Journal of Experimental Education, 56*(2), 77-82.

DeVellis, Robert F. (1991). *Scale development: Theory and applications.* Newbury Park, CA: Sage Publications.

Devlin, Susan J., Dong, H. K., & Brown, Marbue. Selecting a scale for measuring quality. *Marketing Research, 5*(3), 12-17.

Dillman, D. (1972). Increasing mail questionnaire response in large samples of the general public. *Public Opinion Quarterly, 36*(2), 254-257.

Dillman, D., Christenson, J., Carpenter, E., & Brooks, R. (1974). Increasing mail questionnaire response: A four state comparison. *American Sociological Review, 39*, 744-756.

Duncan, W. (1979). Mail questionnaires in survey research: A review of response inducement techniques. *Journal of Management, 5*(1), 39-55.

Enger, John M., Manning, Tom G., Shain, Russell E., Talbert, Lonnie E. & Wright, Donald E. (1993). *Survey questionnaire format effect on response rate and cost per return.* (ERIC Document Reproduction Service No. 358 121)

Foddy, William. (1993). *Constructing survey questions for interviews and questionnaires: Theory and practice in social research.* New York: Cambridge University Press.

Fowler, Floyd J., Jr. (1995). *Improving survey questions: Design and evaluation.* (2nd ed.). Thousand Oaks, CA: Sage Publications.

Fuqua, D., Hartman, B., & Brown, D. (1982). Survey research in higher education. *Research in Higher Education, 17*(1), 69-80.

Gaskell, George D., O'Muircheartaigh, Colm A., & Wright, Daniel B. (1994). Survey questions about the frequency of vaguely defined events: The effects of response alternatives. *Public Opinion Quarterly, 58*, 241-254.

Gawiser, Sheldon R. and Witt, G. Evans. (1994). *A journalist's guide to public opinion polls.* West Port, Connecticut: Praeger.

Goldsmith, R. (1989). Reducing spurious response in a field survey. *Journal of Social Psychology, 129*(2), 201-212.

Groves, Robert M., Cialdini, Robert B., & Couper, Mick P. (1992). Understanding the decision to participate in a survey. *Public Opinion Quarterly, 56*, 475-495.

Heberlein, T. & Baumgartner, R. (1978). Factors affecting response rates to mailed questionnaires: A quantitative analysis of the published literature. *American Sociological Review, 43*(4), 447-462.

189

Hopkins, Kenneth D. (1992). Response rates in survey research: A meta-analysis of the effects of monetary gratuities. *Journal of Experimental Education, 61*(1), 52-62.

Hopkins, Kenneth D., et al. (1988). Mail surveys of professional populations: The effects of monetary gratuities on return rates. *Journal of Experimental Education, 56*(4), 173-175.

Horowitz, J., & Sedlacek, W. (1974). Initial returns on mail questionnaires: A literature review and research note. *Research in Higher Education, 2*(4), 361-367.

Kalton, G., & Kasprzyk, D. (1986). The treatment of missing survey data. *Survey Methodology, 12,* 1-16.

Kanuk, L., & Berenson, C. (1975). Mail surveys and response rates: A literature review. *Journal of Marketing Research, 12*(4), 440-453.

Katz, Elinor. (1993). A critical analysis of interview, telephone, and mail survey design. (ERIC Document Reproduction Service No. 357 069)

Lee, Raymond E. (1993). *Doing research on sensitive topics.* Thousand Oaks, CA: Sage Publications.

Leslie, L. (1972). Are high response rates essential to valid surveys? *Social Science Quarterly, 1,* 323-334.

Lin, I-Fen, & Schaeffer, Nora Cate. (1995). Using survey participants to estimate the impact of nonparticipation. *Public Opinion Quarterly, 59,* 236-258.

Lindsay, M. (1985). Procedures for follow-up studies of teacher education graduates. *Journal of Teacher Education, 36*(2), 29-33.

Linsky, A. (1975). Stimulating responses to mailed questionnaires: A review. *Public Opinion Quarterly, 39*(1), 82-101.

Lodge, Milton. (1981). *Magnitude scaling: Quantitative measurement of opinions.* Beverly Hills, CA: Sage Publications.

Making effective use of mailed questionnaires. (1984, March). (Special Theme Issue). *New Directions for Program Evaluation, 21,* 5-18.

Matross, R. (1981). Uses and abuses of campus opinion polls. *Journal of College Student Personnel, 22,* 114-119.

Ogborne, A., et al. (1986). Dealing with nonrespondents in a mail survey of professionals: The cost-effectiveness of two alternatives. *Evaluation and the Health Professions, 9*(1), 121-128.

Olivia, P. (1976). Survey research: Nuisance or help? *Western Carolina University Journal of Education, 7*(3), 14-17.

Powers, D. & Alderman, D. (1982). Feedback as incentive for responding to a mail questionnaire. *Research in Higher Education, 17*(3), 207-211.

Presser, S., & Blair, J. (1994). Survey pretesting: Do different methods produce different results? *Sociological Methodology.*

Rasinski, Kenneth A., Mingay, David, & Bradburn, Norman M. (1994). Do respondents really "mark all that apply" on self-administered questionnaires? *Public Opinion Quarterly, 58,* 400-408.

Roberson, M. T., & Sundstrom, E. (1990). Questionnaire design, return rates, and response favorableness in an employee attitude questionnaire. *Journal of Applied Psychology, 75*(3), 354-357.

Rubenstein, Sondra M.. (1995). *Surveying public opinion.* Wadsworth Publishing Company.

Rucker, M. & Arbaugh, J. (1979). A comparison of matrix questionnaires with standard questionnaires. *Educational and Psychological Measurement, 39*(3), 637-643.

Schwartz, Norbert, & Hippler, Hans-J. (1995). Subsequent questions may influence answers to preceding questions in mail surveys. *Public Opinion Quarterly, 59,* 93-97.

Senf, J. (1987). The option to refuse: A tool in understanding nonresponse in mailed surveys. *Evaluation Review, 11*(6), 775-781.

Singer, Eleanor, Von Thurn, Dawn R., & Miller, Esther R. (1995). Confidentiality assurances and response: A quantitative review of the experimental literature. *Public Opinion Quarterly, 59,* 66-77.

Smith, K. & Bers, T. (1987). Improving alumni survey response rates: An experiment and cost-benefit analysis. *Research in Higher Education, 27*(3), 218-225.

Spector, Paul E. (1992). *Summated rating scale construction: An introduction.* Newbury Park, CA: Sage Publications.

Trimarco, Paolo. (1994, January). Question the questions: The good, the bad, and the dicey in fund-raising and alumni surveys. *Case Currents,* 32-36.

Wilhoit, G. Cleveland & Weaver, David H. (1990). *Newsroom guide to polls and surveys.* Indiana University Press.

Zaller, John. (1992). *The nature and origin of mass opinion.* New York: Cambridge University Press.

References on Survey Sampling

Cochran, William Gemmell. (1963). *Sampling techniques* (2nd ed.). New York: Wiley.

Fink, Arlene. (1995). *How to sample in surveys.* Thousand Oaks, CA: Sage Publications.

Henry, Gary T. (1990). *Practical sampling.* Thousand Oaks, CA: Sage Publications.

Jaeger, Richard M. (1984). *Sampling in education and the social sciences.* Longman Publications.

Kalton, Graham. (1983). *Introduction to survey sampling.* Thousand Oaks, CA: Sage Publications.

Kish, Leslie. (1965). *Survey sampling.* New York: John Wiley & Sons.

Kraemer, Helena Chmura, & Thiemann, Sue. (1987). *How many subjects? Statistical power analysis in research.* Thousand Oaks, CA: Sage Publications.

Krejcie, R., & Morgan, D. (1970). Determining sample size for research activities. *Educational and Psychological Measurement, 30,* 607-610.

Lee, Eun Sul, Forthofer, Ronald N., & Lorimor, Ronald J. (1989). *Analyzing complex survey data.* Thousand Oaks, CA: Sage Publications.

Scheaffer, Richard L., Mendenhall, William, & Ott, Lyman. (1990). *Elementary survey sampling* (4th ed.). Boston: PWS-Kent Publishing Co.

Sudman, Seymour. (1976). *Applied sampling.* New York: Academic Press.

Williams, B. (1978). *A sampler of sampling.* New York: John Wiley & Sons.

References on Reliability and Validity

Biemer, P., Groves, R., Lyberg, L, Mathiowetz, N., & Sudman, S. (Eds.). (1991). *Measurement errors in surveys.* New York: John Wiley & Sons.

Campbell, D. F., & Fiske, D. W. (1959). Convergent and discriminant validation by the multitrait-multimethod matrix. *Psychological Bulletin, 56,* 81-105.

Dick, Walter, & Hagerty, Nancy. (1971). *Topics in measurement: Reliability and validity.* New York: McGraw-Hill.

Garmines, Edward G., & Zeller, Richard A. (1979). *Reliability and validity assessment.* Beverly Hills: Sage Publications.

Gronlund, Norman E. (1990). *Measurement and evaluation in teaching* (6th ed.). New York: Macmillan Publishing Company.

Groves, Robert M. (1989). *Survey errors and survey costs.* New York: Wiley.

Jacobs, Lucy Chester, & Chase, Clinton I. (1992). *Developing and using tests effectively: A guide for faculty.* San Francisco: Jossey-Bass.

Litwin, Mark S. (1995). *How to measure survey reliability and validity.* Thousand Oaks, CA: Sage Publications.

Malhotra, Naersh K. (1992). On the construct validity of intrinsic sources of personal relevance. *Journal of Business Research, 23,* 143-147.

Mehrens, William A., & Lehmann, Irvin J. (1991). *Measurement and evaluation in education and psychology* (4th ed.). Fort Worth: Harcourt Brace College Publishers.

Peter, J. Paul. (1979). Reliability: A review of psychometric basics and recent marketing practices. *Journal of Marketing Research, 16,* 6-17.

Peter, J. Paul. (1981). Construct validity: A review of basic issues and marketing practices. *Journal of Marketing Research, 18,* 133-145.

Peter, J. Paul, & Churchill, Gilbert A., Jr. (1986). Relationships among research design choices and psychometric properties of rating scales: A meta-analysis. *Journal of Marketing Research, 23,* 1-10.

Schwarz, Norbert, & Sudman, Seymour (Eds.). (1994). *Autobiographical memory and the validity of retrospective reports.* New York: Springer Verlag.

Takalar, P., Waugh, G., & Micceri, T. (1993, May). *A search for TRUTH in student responses to selected survey items.* Paper presented at the Annual Forum of the Association for Institutional Research, Chicago.

Wentland, Ellen J., & Smith, Kent W. (1993). *Survey responses: An evaluation of their validity.* San Diego: Academic Press.

References on Telephone Surveys

Blankenship, A. B. (1977). *Professional telephone surveys.* New York: McGraw-Hill.

Connor, Martha. (1995, July-August). Dialing for data. *Case Currents, 21*(7), 44-48.

Dillman, Donald. (1978). *Mail and telephone surveys: The total design method.* New York: John Wiley & Sons.

Frey, James H. (1989). *Survey research by telephone* (2nd ed.). Newbury Park, CA: Sage Publications.

Frey, James H., & Oishi, Sabine Mertens. (1995). *How to conduct interviews by telephone and in person.* Thousand Oaks, CA: Sage Publications.

Groves, R. M., Biemer, P. P., Lyberg, L. E., Massey, J. T., Nicholls II, W. L., & Waksberg, J. (Eds.). (1988). *Telephone survey methodology.* New York: John Wiley & Sons.

Groves, R., & Kahn, R. (1979). *Surveys by telephone: A national comparison with personal interviews.* Orlando: Academic Press.

Ibsen, C. A., & Ballweg, J. A. (1974). Telephone interviews in social research: Some methodological considerations. *Quality and Quantity, 8,* 181-192.

Lavrakas, Paul J. (1993). *Telephone survey methods: Sampling, selection and supervision* (2nd ed.). Thousand Oaks, CA: Sage Publications.

Massey, J. T., Nicholls II, W. L., & Waksberg, J. (Eds.). (1988). *Telephone survey methodology.* New York: John Wiley & Sons.

Oldendick, Robert W., & Link, Michael W. (1994, Summer). The answering machine generation: Who are they and what problem do they pose for survey research? *Public Opinion Quarterly, 58,* 264-273.

Tuckel, Peter S., & Feinberg, Barry M. (1991, Summer). The answering machine poses many questions for telephone survey researchers. *Public Opinion Quarterly, 55* (2), 200-217.

References on Focus Groups

Bers, Trudy H. (1987). Exploring institutional images through focus group interviews. In Lay, Robert S., & Endo, Jean (Eds.), *Designing and Using Market Research, 54,* 19-29. San Francisco: Jossey-Bass.

Bers, Trudy H. (1989). The popularity and problems of focus-group research. *College and University, 64,* 260-268.

Bers, Trudy H., and Smith, K. (1988, Spring). Focus groups and community college research: Lessons from a study of nontraditional students. *Community College Review, 15*(4), 52-58.

Brewer, J., & Hunter, A. (1989). *Multimethod research: A synthesis of styles.* Newbury Park, CA: Sage Publications.

Calder, B. J. (1984). Focus groups and the nature of qualitative marketing research. *Journal of Marketing Research,* 39-44.

Goodman, R. I. (1984). Focus group interviews in media product testing. *Educational Technology, 24,* 39-44.

Greenbaum, Thomas L. (1988). *The practical handbook and guide to focus group research.* Lexington, MA: D. C. Heath.

Krueger, Richard A. (1994). *Focus groups: A practical guide for applied research* (2nd ed.). Thousand Oaks, CA: Sage Publications.

Morgan, David L. (1988). *Focus groups as qualitative research.* Newbury Park, CA: Sage Publications.

Morgan, David L. (Ed.) (1993). *Successful focus groups: Advancing the state of the art.* Newbury Park, CA: Sage Publications.

Stewart, David W., & Shamdasani, Prem N. (1990). *Focus groups: Theory and practice.* Newbury Park, CA: Sage Publications.

References on Statistical Analysis

Agresti, Alan & Agresti, Barbara F. (1979) *Statistical methods for the social sciences.* Dellen Publishing Company.

Binder, Arnold. (1984). Restrictions on statistics imposed by method of measurement: Some reality, some myth. *Journal of Criminal Justice, 12,* 467-481.

Bohrnstedt, George W. & Knoke, David. (1994). *Statistics for social data analysis* (3rd ed.). F.E. Peacock Publishers.

Cleveland, William S. (1993). *Visualizing data.* Murray Hill, New Jersey: Hobart Press.

Clogg, Clifford C., & Shihadeh, Edward S. (1994). *Statistical models for ordinal variables.* Thousand Oaks, CA: Sage Publications.

Cohen, Jacob & Cohen, Patricia. (1983). *Applied multiple regression/correlation analysis for the behavioral sciences.* Hillsdale, New Jersey: L. Erlbaum Associates.

Dillon, W. R., & Goldstein, M. (1984). *Multivariate analysis methods and applications.* New York: Wiley & Sons.

Fink, Arlene. (1995). *How to analyze survey data.* Thousand Oaks, CA: Sage Publications.

Fitz-Gibbon, C., & Morris, L. (1987). *How to analyze data.* Newbury Park: Sage Publications.

Gaito, John. (1980). Measurement scales and statistics: Resurgence of an old misconception. *Psychological Bulletin, 87,* 564-567.

Gaito, John. (1984). Measurement scales and statistics: A confusion which refuses to die. *Canadian Psychology, 25,* 249-250.

Gaito, John. (1986). Some issues in the measurement-statistics controversy. *Canadian Psychology, 27,* 63-68.

Gonick, Larry, & Smith, Woollcott. (1993). *A cartoon guide to statistics.* New York: HarperCollins Publishers.

Hanushek, Eric & Jackson, John. (1977). *Statistical methods for social scientists.* Orlando: Academic Press.

Hays, William L. (1988). *Statistics* (4th ed.). San Francisco: Harcourt Brace Jovanovich.

Healey, Joseph. (1996). *Statistics: Tools for social research.* Wadsworth Publishing Company.

Jaeger, Richard M. (1990). *Statistics: A spectator sport* (2nd ed.). Thousand Oaks, CA: Sage Publications.

Judd, Charles M. & McClelland, Gary H. (1990). *Data analysis: A model-comparison approach.* San Diego: Harcourt Brace Jovanovich.

Kanji, Gopal K. (1993). *100 statistical tests.* Thousand Oaks, CA: Sage Publications.

Leach, Chris. (1979). *Introduction to statistics: A nonparametric approach for the social sciences.* New York: John Wiley & Sons.

Likert, Rensis. (1932, June). A technique for the measurement of attitudes. *Archives of Psychology, 140.*

Mauro, John. (1992). *Statistical deception at work.* Hillsdale, New Jersey: L. Erlbaum Associates.

Micceri, Theodore. (1990). *Feel no guilt! Your statistics are probably robust.* (ERIC Document Reproduction Service No. ED 317 601).

Noether, G. E. (1991). *Introduction to statistics: The nonparametric way.* New York: Springer-Verlag.

Norman, Geoffrey R., & Streiner, David L. (1986). *PDQ Statistics.* Toronto: B. C. Decker, Inc.

Pedhazur, E. J. (1982). *Multiple regression in behavioral research: Explanations and prediction* (2nd ed.). New York: Holt, Rinehart, & Winston.

Sirkin, R. Mark. (1994). *Statistics for the social sciences.* Thousand Oaks, CA: Sage Publications.

Stevens, S. S. (1946). On the theory of scales of measurement. *Science, 103,* 677-680.

Stevens, S. S. (1968). Measurement, statistics, and the schemapiric view. *Science, 161,* 849-856.

Tabachnik, Barbara G. & Fidell, Linda S. (1995). *Using multivariate statistics.* Harper Collins College.

Tatsuoska, M. M. (1971). *Multivariate analysis: Techniques for educational and psychological research.* New York: Wiley & Sons.

Traylor, Mark. (1983). Ordinal and interval scaling. *Journal of the Market Research Society, 25,* 297-303.

Velleman, Paul F., & Wilkinson, Leland. (1993). Nominal, ordinal, interval, and ratio typologies are misleading. *American Statistician, 47,* 65-72.

Wonnacott, Ronald J. & Wonnacott, Thomas H. *Introductory statistics* (5th ed.). New York: John Wiley & Sons.

Yancey, B. D. (Ed.). (1988). *Applying statistics in institutional research.* New Directions for Institutional Research No. 58. San Francisco: Jossey-Bass.

Yancey, B. D., & Ruddock, M. S. (1987). Using statistical packages/spreadsheets. In J. A. Muffo & G. W. McLaughlin (Eds.), *A Primer on Institutional Research.* Tallahassee, FL: Association for Institutional Research.

Zumbo, Bruno D., & Zimmerman, Donald W. (1993). Is the selection of statistical methods governed by level of measurement? *Canadian Psychology, 34,* 390-399.

References on Qualitative Data Analysis

Bogdan, R. C., & Biklen, S. K. (1992). *Qualitative research for education.* Boston: Allyn & Bacon.

Denzin, Norman K. & Lincoln, Yvonna S. (Eds.). (1994). *Handbook of qualitative research.* Thousand Oaks, CA: Sage Publications.

Dey, I. (1993). *Qualitative data analysis: A user-friendly guide for social scientists.* London: Routledge.

Fielding, N. G. & Lee, R. N. (1991). *Using computers in qualitative research.* Newbury Park, CA: Sage Publications.

Huberman, A. Michael & Richards, Lyn. (1994). Data management and analysis methods. In Norman K. Denzin & Yvonna S. Lincoln (Eds.), *Handbook of qualitative research.* Thousand Oaks, CA: Sage Publications.

Marshall, Catherine, & Rossman, Gretchen B. (1994). *Designing qualitative research* (2nd ed.). Thousand Oaks, CA: Sage Publications.

Morse, Janice M., & Field, Peggy Anne. (1995). *Qualitative research methods* (2nd ed.). Thousand Oaks, CA: Sage Publications.

Patton, M. Q. (1990). *Qualitative evaluation and research methods.* Newbury Park, CA: Sage Publications.

Richards, Thomas J. & Richards, Lyn. (1994). Using computers in qualitative research. In Norman K. Denzin & Yvonna S. Lincoln (Eds.), *Handbook of qualitative research.* Thousand Oaks, CA: Sage Publications.

Silverman, David. (1993). *Interpreting qualitative data: Methods for analyzing talk, text, and interaction.* Thousand Oaks, CA: Sage Publications.

Strauss, Anselm, & Corbin, Juliet. (1990). *Basics of qualitative research: Grounded theory, procedures & techniques.* Newbury Park, CA: Sage Publications.

Wolcott, Harry F. (1994). *Transforming qualitative data: Description, analysis, and interpretation.* Thousand Oaks, CA: Sage Publications.

References on Qualitative Data Analysis Software

Booth, S. (1993). Computer-assisted analysis in qualitative research. *Computers in Human Behavior, 9,* 203-211.

Franzosi, R. (1990). Computer-assisted coding of textual data. *Sociological Methods and Research, 19.*

Kelle, Udo (Ed.). (1995). *Computer-aided qualitative research.* Thousand Oaks, CA: Sage Publications.

Miles, Matthew B., & Huberman, A. Michael. (1994). *Qualitative data analysis: An expanded sourcebook* (2nd ed.). Thousand Oaks, CA: Sage Publications.

Qualitative Sociology, especially Volume 7 (1 and 2) from 1984 and Volume 14 (3 and 4) from 1991.

Stiles, William. (1992). *Describing talk.* Newbury Park, CA: Sage Publications.

Tesch, Renata. (1990). *Qualitative research.* Taylor and Francis.

Tesch, Renata. (1991). Software for qualitative researchers: Analysis needs and program capabilities. In Fielding, N., & Lee, R. (Eds.), *Using computers in qualitative research.* London: Sage Publications.

Weitzman, Eben A., & Miles, Matthew B. (1995). *Computer programs for qualitative data analysis: A software sourcebook.* Thousand Oaks, CA: Sage Publications.

References on Preparing Reports and Presentations

Brody, Marjorie, & Kent, Shawn. (1992). *Power business presentations: How to connect with your audience and sell your ideas.* New York: John Wiley & Sons.

Cleveland, W. S. (1985). *The elements of graphing data.* Boston: Duxbury.

Dewdney, A. K. (1993). *200% of nothing.* New York: John Wiley & Sons.

Hartley, James. (1992, June-July). A postscript to Wainer's "Understanding graphs and tables." *Educational Researcher, 21*(5), 25-26.

Hartley, James. (1991). Tabling information. *American Psychologist, 46*(6), 655-656.

Hartley, James. (1991). Presenting visual information orally. *Information Design Journal, 6* 211-220.

Heller, F. (Ed.) (1986). *The use and abuse of social science.* London: Sage Publications.

Henry, Gary T. (1994). *Graphing data: Techniques for display and analysis.* Thousand Oaks, CA: Sage Publications.

Jaffe, A. J., & Spirer, H. F. (1986). *Misused statistics: Straight talk for twisted numbers.* Marcel Dekker.

Leech, Thomas. (1992). *How to prepare, stage, & deliver winning presentations.* AMA Books.

Meier, N. H. (1991). *The data game: Controversies in social science statistics.* Armonk, NY: M. E. Sharp, Inc.

Morris, Lynn Lyons, Fitz-Gibbon, Carol Taylor, & Freeman, Marie E. (1987). *How to communicate evaluation findings.* Newbury Park: Sage Publications.

Peoples, David. (1992). *Presentations plus: David Peoples' proven techniques* (2nd ed.). New York: John Wiley & Sons.

Richardson, L. (1990). *Writing strategies: Reaching diverse audiences.* Newbury Park, CA: Sage Publications.

Tufte, E. R. (1983). *The visual display of quantitative information.* Cheshire, CT: Graphics Press.

Wainer, Howard. (1984). How to display data badly. *The American Statistician, 38,* 137-147.

Wainer, Howard. (1992, January-February). Understanding graphs and tables. *Educational Researcher, 21*(1), 14-23.

Wainer, Howard. (1993). Making readable overhead displays. *Chance: New Directions for Statistics and Computing, 6* (2), 46-49.

Will-Harris, Daniel. (1995, June). Ask Dr. Daniel: How do I convey my message more clearly? *WordPerfect for Windows Magazine*, 63-66.

Wolcott, H. F. (1990). *Writing up qualitative research.* Newbury Park, CA: Sage Publications.

Information Available via the Internet: Discussion Lists

Unless otherwise noted, to subscribe to any of these discussion lists, send the following message (no subject) to listserv@[list address]:

> subscribe [listname] [firstname] [lastname]

For example, to subscribe to the Methods list, send the following message (no subject) to listserv@unmvma.unm.edu:

> subscribe methods firstname lastname

Academic Research in Marketing:
ELMAR@COLUMBIA.EDU
Send subscription message to ELMAR-REQUEST@COLUMBIA.EDU.

American Educational Research Association Division D: Measurement & Research Methodology:
AERA-D@ASUVM.INRE.ASU.EDU

American Educational Research Association Division J: Postsecondary Education:
AERA-J@ASUVM.INRE.ASU.EDU

Assessment in Higher Education:
ASSESS@LSV.UKY.EDU

Association for Institutional Research (AIR) Discussion of College Rankings, Guidebooks, and Reputational Studies:
RANK-L@ABACUS.BATES.EDU

Association for Institutional Research (AIR) Discussion of Standard Survey Response Forms:
STAND-L@ABACUS.BATES.EDU

Minitab:
MINITAB@MAILBASE.AC.UK

Psychological Measure Development, Testing, and Validation:
VALIDATA@UA1VM.UA.EDU

Public Opinion Research:
POR@UNC.EDU

Qualitative Methods:
QUAL-L@PSUVM.BITNET

Qualitative Research:
QUAL-RS@UGA.CC.UGA.EDU
QUALNET@CHIMERA.SPH.UMN.EDU

Qualitative Research/Text-Based Analysis Software Packages:
QUAL-SOFTWARE@MAILBASE.AC.UK
Send subscription message
join qual-software yourfirstname yourlastname
to MAILBASE@MAILBASE.AC.UK

SAS:
SAS-L@UGA.CC.UGA.EDU

SAS Public Access Consortium:
SASPAC-L@VTVM1.CC.VT.EDU

Social Science Research Methods Instructors:
METHODS@UNMVMA.UNM.EDU

Software Role and Use in Institutional Research:
IR-SOFT-L@WILLAMETTE.EDU
Send subscription message to LISTPROC@WILLAMETTE.EDU

SPSS-X:
SPSSX-L@UGA.CC.UGA.EDU
SUPPORT@SPSS.COM

Statistical Consulting:
STAT-L@VM1.MCGILL.CA

Systat:
SYSTAT-L@UICVM.BITNET

Teaching and Learning of Statistics:
EDSTAT-L@JSE.STAT.NCSU.EDU

Information Available via the Internet: World Wide Web Sites

At the rate the World Wide Web is growing, by the time you read this the number of home pages of interest to survey researchers has probably grown a hundredfold. Here, then, are just a few sites to get you started:

American Educational Research Association (AERA):
http://tikkun.ed.asu.edu/aera/home.html

Assessment and Evaluation on the Internet:
http://www.cua.edu/www/eric_ae/intass.html

BMDP:
http://www.bmdp.com/

Center for Social Science Computation & Research:
http://augustus.csscr.washington.edu

The Chance Project (dedicated to improving the quality of statistics education):
http://www.geom.umn.edu/locate/chance

Educational Resources Information Center (ERIC):
http://www.aspensys.com/eric/index.html

Educational Resources Information Center (ERIC) Clearinghouse on Assessment and Evaluation:
http://www.cua.edu/www/eric_ae

Educational Resources Information Center (ERIC) Adjunct Test Collection Clearinghouse:
gopher://vmsgopher.cua.edu.:70/11gopher_root_eric_ae:[_tc]

Epi Info:
http://mkn.co.uk/help/extra/people/Brixton_Books

Internet Resources for Institutional Research:
http://apollo.gmu.edu/~jmilam/air95.html#air

Journal of Statistics Education:
http://www2.ncsu.edu/ncsu/pams/stat/info/jse/homepage.html

Journal of Statistics Education Information Service:
gopher://jse.stat.ncsu.edu:70/1/

Minitab:
http://www.minitab.com/

National Center for Research on Evaluation, Standards, and Student Testing (CRESST):
http://www.cse.ucla.edu/CRESSTHome.html

National Council of Measurement in Education:
http://www.assessment.iupui.edu/NCME/NCME.html

Outcomes Assessment:
http://spot.colorado.edu/~schechte/outcomes.htm

Questionnaire Programming Language:
http://www.gao.gov/qpl/qpl.htm

Research Methods:
http://www.helsinki.fi/valttdk/atk/stat/links.html

Research Methods Resources:
http://seamonkey.ed.asu.edu/~behrens/

SAS:
http://www.sas.com/

Social Science Research Methods and Statistics: Resources for Teachers:
http://www.siu.edu/~hawkes/methods.html

Social Science Software Databank SIByl:
http://www.gamma.rug.nl/sibhome.html

SPSS:
http://www.spss.com/

Statistics:
http://maddog.fammed.wisc.edu/~helberg/statistics.html
http://www.stat.ucla.edu/textbook/

World Wide Web Virtual Library in Education:
http://www.csu.edu.au/education/library.html

World Wide Web Virtual Library in the Social Sciences:
http://www.coombs.anu.edu.au/WWWVL-SocSci.html

Information Available via Organizations, Groups, and Programs

The American Association on Public Opinion Research (AAPOR). For information, contact Catherine Ostrowski, AAPOR Administrator, P. O. Box 1248, Ann Arbor, MI 48106, telephone (313) 764-1555.

The Joint Program in Survey Methodology sponsored by the University of Maryland and the University of Michigan. For information, contact the Joint Program in Survey Methodology, University of Michigan, P.O. Box 1248, Ann Arbor, MI 48106-1248, telephone (800) 937-9320, or the Joint Program in Survey Methodology, University of Maryland, 1218 Lefrak Hall, College Park, MD 20742, telephone (301) 314-7911.

Clearinghouse for Higher Education Assessment Instruments. For information, contact the Clearinghouse for Higher Education Assessment Instruments, The University of Tennessee, Knoxville, 212 Claxton Education Building, Knoxville, TN 37996-3400, telephone (615) 974-3748.